C000264476

LIV
DIFFEREN
TO MAK
DIFFEREN

The Bible Reading Fellowship
15 The Chambers, Vineyard
Abingdon OX14 3FE
brf.org.uk

The Bible Reading Fellowship (BRF) is a Registered Charity (233280)

ISBN 978 0 85746 671 6
First published 2018
10 9 8 7 6 5 4 3 2 1 0
All rights reserved

Text © Will Donaldson 2018
This edition © The Bible Reading Fellowship 2018
Cover image © John Davis/Stocktrek Images/Getty

The author asserts the moral right to be identified as the author of this work

Acknowledgements
Unless otherwise acknowledged, scripture quotations are from The Holy Bible, New
International Version (Anglicised edition) copyright © 1979, 1984, 2011 by Biblica.
Used by permission of Hodder & Stoughton Publishers, a Hachette UK company.
All rights reserved. 'NIV' is a registered trademark of Biblica. UK trademark number
1448790.

Scripture quotations from The New Revised Standard Version of the Bible, Anglicised
edition, copyright © 1989, 1995 by the Division of Christian Education of the National
Council of the Churches of Christ in the United States of America. Used by permission.
All rights reserved.

Extracts from the Authorised Version of the Bible (The King James Bible), the rights
in which are vested in the Crown, are reproduced by permission of the Crown's
Patentee, Cambridge University Press.

Every effort has been made to trace and contact copyright owners for material used
in this resource. We apologise for any inadvertent omissions or errors, and would
ask those concerned to contact us so that full acknowledgement can be made in
the future.

A catalogue record for this book is available from the British Library

Printed and bound by CPI Group (UK) Ltd, Croydon CR0 4YY

LIVING DIFFERENTLY TO MAKE A DIFFERENCE

THE BEATITUDES AND COUNTERCULTURAL LIFESTYLE

WILL DONALDSON

Dedicated in memory of Brian Miller and Mike Stocks,
both called home early, with deep gratitude
for all they invested in their children.

CONTENTS

FOREWORD

Matthew takes great care in setting out the teaching of Jesus in five sections of the gospel. The first and the longest is the sermon on the mount. At the head of the sermon on the mount, with almost the first words of Jesus in this gospel, Matthew sets the beautiful sayings beginning with 'Blessed': the inexhaustible beatitudes. They are a kind of manifesto (and a manifesto of kindness).

There are signs that the beatitudes are coming back into focus in the life of the church as a text for the 21st century. They are pithy and memorable. Each one can fit into a tweet, yet each is like clicking on an icon: exploring even a single word unlocks many layers of the biblical tradition. In the Diocese of Oxford, we are part way through a whole year of asking every church, chaplaincy and school – and every Christian – to set these words of Jesus at the centre of what it means to be the church. We are trying to knead the beatitudes through the life of the church as a baker kneads yeast through dough, and we are waiting to see what good things will emerge for the kingdom of God.

Will Donaldson has written a clear, deep and practical guide to living the beatitudes for every disciple. The book's focus is not simply on understanding the text but on living in this way as a disciple and as part of a community of disciples: the church. As we read and study and live this text, so we see more clearly, as Will argues, the face behind the beatitudes: the self-portrait of the one who, long ago, walked up the mountain and began to teach his disciples and, in that teaching, began to change the world.

Rt Revd Dr Steven Croft
Bishop of Oxford

INTRODUCTION: UNHEALTHY LIFESTYLES

This morning I watched a young doctor on BBC Breakfast TV offer a solution to the overstretched and underfunded UK National Health Service (NHS), which is fast approaching breaking point. Dr Rangan Chatterjee, a GP from Oldham in Greater Manchester and an established thought leader in the field of preventive medicine, has focused on 'lifestyle medicine'. He argued that the NHS is in crisis largely owing to unhealthy lifestyles, such as poor diet, smoking, low levels of physical activity, excess alcohol and extremely high stress levels. These factors now fuel the majority of global deaths and diseases. To quote from his blog:

> Our training (as doctors) is not as useful for the current epidemic of chronic lifestyle-related conditions that are now flooding our surgeries. I focus on finding the root cause of diseases and help my patients make their illnesses disappear.[1]

A BBC1 documentary, called *Doctor in the House*, follows Dr Chatterjee as he is allowed into the homes of sick patients to assess their lifestyles during the day and night over the period of a few weeks. Dr Chatterjee says: 'I stayed 13 full days with them, spread over a period of seven weeks so that I could immerse myself in their lifestyle and see the kind of foods they were eating. I also stayed two nights to monitor their sleep patterns and what they were doing to wind down'.[2] He then offers them a diagnosis, with a prescription of lifestyle changes rather than prescription pills.

Dr Chatterjee comes up with a series of steps to better health, which, put concisely, are 'eat, move, sleep, relax'. Dr Aseem Malhotra, consultant cardiologist and advisor to the National Obesity Forum, agrees with him:

> Our current NHS crisis is the product of a broken system rooted in too many prescription medications of dubious benefit that come with side effects combined with unhealthy lifestyles resulting in a public health disaster... The future of sustainable healthcare will require taking less drugs and utilising more lifestyle interventions, which will not only save the NHS billions but improve the quality of life for millions of UK citizens.[3]

What if the unhealthy lifestyle problems facing the NHS are a reflection of the wider social and spiritual problems facing the whole of the world today? Despite all the advances in science, medicine, technology, social care and human rights – and they are significant – we live in what can only be described as a wounded and broken world. The range of problems facing our global community seems bigger than ever, beyond the capacity of any leaders or organisations to sort out. Globalisation seems to have failed to deliver the quality of life that it promised and has left many disillusioned and marginalised. Consumerism and materialism have not provided the inner contentment and satisfaction that they promised, but have only deepened the sense of the emptiness of life. As the scientific and rationalistic certainties of the modern era have given way to the uncertainties and scepticism of the postmodern world, people have been left wondering whether there is any meaning or purpose in life at all, causing a profound sense of lostness. A distressed student expressed exactly that to me last week with chilling clarity in a pastoral encounter.

The financial systems of many nations have collapsed or are in long-term deficit. Environmental concerns continue to grow in severity as governments repeatedly fail to deliver their national targets. International tensions continue to escalate between the West and Russia, the US and North Korea, and regional struggles persist in the Middle East. Serious terrorist strikes have put European capitals on high alert with alarming frequency. Millions in developing nations live in abject poverty, lacking the basic necessities of food, clothing, clean water, shelter, healthcare and education. Family life and marriages throughout Europe are under pressure, and there is a staggering rise in mental health problems among children and young people. Our prisons in the UK are overfull and understaffed, and drugs and violence are commonplace among the inmates, with high levels of reoffending after release. There has been a relentless media exposure of celebrities, politicians and church leaders who have abused children and young people to suit their own selfish pleasures.

In addition, technology and robotics, for all their blessings, can have dehumanising, disempowering and destructive effects. The dark side of the internet is well known, with a billion-dollar pornography industry that exploits and dehumanises those involved, and with terrorist websites that radicalise vulnerable young people. Social media has a dark side too, with cyber bullying, paedophile grooming and sexting very common among children and young people.

Yuval Noah Harari is an Israeli academic who is trying to look into the future and predict how the human race is evolving, particularly in the light of our growing dependence on computers, smartphones and robots. In his latest book, *Homo Deus*, he says: 'We increasingly outsource mental and communicative activities to computers. We are merging with our smartphones.'[4] He believes this has political as well as personal ramifications, with power to rule moving to those who know about algorithms and biotechnology, and who have the ability to process information centrally, because they will be able to 'construct a total surveillance regime that follows every individual all the time', including phone calls, emails and movements.

As regards robotics, they are mainly being used at present in work situations where there is a danger to human life, such as bomb disposal or manufacturing industries. But, in Japan, robots have much more developed and controversial roles: as companions for humans, especially the elderly, as sexual partners or entertainment bots, even as humanoids hired as priests to take funerals, chanting Buddhist sutras in a computerised voice. There is also the extremely worrying dimension of cyberattacks and cybercrime, brought centre stage by two recent major cyberattacks that targeted operating systems used by many businesses. A report published by the insurance market Lloyds of London warned that the financial implications of a major incident could be as high as $121 billion, based on the worst-case impact of a 'malicious attack that takes down a cloud service provider' having knock-on effects for many other businesses.

Another perspective of our Western brokenness is poignantly documented in *Hillbilly Elegy: A memoir of a family and culture in crisis* by J.D. Vance.[5] Vance grew up in white, working-class communities in Ohio and Kentucky and, after leaving high school, served in the Marine Corps in Iraq, became a graduate of Yale Law School and now works as an investor in a leading venture capital firm, writing occasionally for *The New York Times* and the *National Review*. His personal story charts the social decline of his family and community, and provides a troubling meditation on the loss of the American Dream for a large segment of the population.

What if all these social, political and technological problems were connected to the same fundamental root cause: a chronic lifestyle dysfunction? What if Oswald J. Smith was right when he said: 'The heart of the human problem, is the problem of the human heart'? What if Archbishop Thomas Cranmer was not overstating the seriousness of the human condition and the state of our souls in his prayer of confession in the Church of England's Prayer Book?

> Almighty and most merciful Father, we have erred, and strayed from thy ways like lost sheep. We have followed too much the devices and desires of our own hearts. We have offended against thy holy laws. We have left undone those things which we ought to have done; and we have done those things which we ought not to have done; and there is no health in us.[6]

What if, despite being fearfully and wonderfully made in the image of God, and being capable of lofty heights in the arts and sciences, music and culture, literature and sport, kindness and compassion, there is – at the end of the day – 'no health in us'?

Then we would need a doctor, a divine physician of the soul. Then we would need a 'doctor in the house' who would enter our world and come and live alongside us, and observe the dysfunction of our lives and give us a truthful diagnosis about the way we need to change our lifestyles.

And what if the God of heaven has indeed sent a divine physician, a Saviour, a practitioner in the healing of souls? What if he was the one about whom John said: 'The Word became flesh and made his dwelling among us… full of grace and truth' (John 1:14)? What if he said to those who would listen to him: 'It is not the healthy who need a doctor, but those who are ill. I have not come to call the righteous, but sinners to repentance' (Luke 5:31–32). What if coming under his lordship and rule over our lives brought the healing and peace we so desperately wanted, as he indicated in Matthew 11:29: 'Take my yoke upon you and learn from me, for I am gentle and humble in heart, and you will find rest for your souls.' What if the restoring of our souls was only a small part in a much bigger plan to 'make all things new' (Revelation 21:5), putting the world to rights, creating a new heaven and earth?

Then there would be hope. But for that hope to be realised there would need to be, firstly, a careful listening to his diagnosis; then, a personal application of his prescription; and, finally, a daily attentiveness to his teaching, adjusting our lifestyles to his ways.

This book invites us on that journey of healing, the reordering of our lives around the central call of Jesus to discipleship in the beatitudes. John Stott, in his commentary on the sermon on the mount entitled *Christian Counter-Culture*, helpfully described them as follows:

> The Beatitudes set forth the balanced and variegated character of Christian people... they are Christ's own specification of what every Christian ought to be. All the qualities are to characterise all of his followers... they are his ideal for every citizen of God's Kingdom... they paint a comprehensive portrait of a Christian disciple.[7]

They are strategically placed at the entrance of the sermon on the mount, so they provide the necessary gateway through which all should enter this world-famous treatise. The beatitudes are giving us the principles and values that will be illustrated and worked out in practice in the various sections of the sermon. In doing this, Jesus is announcing the arrival of the messianic kingdom, foretold in the Old Testament, and fulfilled in his own life and ministry. So, the New Cambridge Bible Commentary on Matthew by Craig Evans, distinguished Professor of New Testament at Acadia Divinity School in Nova Scotia, highlights the importance of the beatitudes in terms of their being a proclamation of his messianic kingdom: 'One of the striking features of Jesus' beatitudes is the many parallels with Isaiah 61:1–11.'[8] In this, he is following the scholarly work of Davies and Allison, who identify very similar allusions to Isaiah 61, concluding: 'If, as seems overwhelmingly probable, the core of the beatitudes... be dominical, Jesus must have formulated them with Isaiah 61:1–3 in mind... the influence of Isaiah 61 should be located at the fount of this tradition.'[9]

Isaiah 61 was the Old Testament passage that Jesus read in the synagogue at Nazareth to announce the arrival of the Messiah, and he finished with those explosive words: 'Today this scripture is fulfilled in your hearing' (Luke 4:21); and Isaiah 61 is heavily alluded to in his reply to John the Baptist's disciples who come to him and ask: 'Are you the one who is to come, or should we expect someone else?' (Luke 7:20). And Jesus' reply is, in effect: 'Take a look at what is going on; does this not look like Isaiah 61? Of course I am the Messiah!' However, here too in the beatitudes, Craig Evans finds no fewer than seven deliberate allusions to Isaiah 61 and we shall note these – and more – when we get to them individually. But the point to grasp is that Jesus, in the beatitudes, is once again announcing the arrival of the messianic kingdom, foreshadowed in Isaiah 61 and now fulfilled in their very hearing. This is a messianic manifesto – setting out which kind of people are and will be part of it, and what it means to live under the just and gentle rule of the anointed Christ.

The beatitudes have also been very important in the history of the church. Robert Warren, in his book on the beatitudes, makes this point while lamenting the fact that the church seems to have lost sight of them recently:

> In the early Christian centuries they were one of the key texts for those being initiated into the faith, alongside the Lord's Prayer and the Creed. Those three texts helped newcomers to the faith to know what to believe (the Creed), how to pray (the Lord's Prayer) and how to live (the Beatitudes)... for much of the history of the church they have been the roots from which Christian spirituality, moral behaviour, and discipleship have been nourished and inspired.[10]

More than that, we shall see the beatitudes being embodied in Jesus' own life and ministry, brought to us by the gospel narratives. So, in this sense, they express who he was, what he valued, and how he behaved. In calling us to live them out, he is really calling us to follow his example, to be Christlike in who we are, what we value and how we live. John Stott's last speaking engagement before retiring from public ministry at the age of 86 was at the 2007 Keswick Convention. During it he said:

> What is God's purpose for his people?... I want to share with you where my mind has come to rest as I approach the end of my pilgrimage on earth, and it is – God wants his people to become like Christ. Christlikeness is the will of God for the people of God.[11]

He supported this statement persuasively with three key texts – Romans 8:29, 2 Corinthians 3:18 and 1 John 3:2 – and it was unarguably conclusive and profound. But he might have chosen Matthew 5:1–10 as a call to Christlikeness, for this is a lesson from Jesus himself in how to live like him and imitate the beauty of his life.

In this way, Christ is also calling us to be countercultural, to be different from a world that has a completely different set of values. Dr R.T. France, in his magisterial commentary on Matthew, says: 'His committed disciples… are called to a radically new lifestyle, in conscious distinction from the norms of the society. They are to be an alternative society, a Christian counterculture.'[12] The world might say: Blessed are the strong, the ones who exercise the force of their character, the ones who aggressively assert themselves, the ones who climb the ladder, the rich and powerful, the ones who know how to manipulate the system, the ones who are willing to trample over others to get ahead. It is a view of the world as a jungle and it is all about the survival of the fittest. But none of this is found in the beatitudes. In fact, not only are these kinds of values conspicuously absent, but the opposite kinds of values are being exalted and exemplified. It is the poor, the meek, the merciful and peacemakers who show that they are God's people.

So this is where the beatitudes will take us: they will enable us to become more like Christ and, at the same time, allow us to be different, marked out from the world in order that we can be salt and light (Matthew 5:13–14), influencing society with the values of heaven, effecting change for the kingdom of God, and bearing witness to the reality and beauty of our heavenly Father. It is a call to be different in order to make a difference.

In *The Christ of the Indian Road* by the missionary E. Stanley Jones, the author asked Gandhi how to naturalise Christianity into India. Gandhi replied: 'I would suggest first of all that all of you Christians… begin to live more like Jesus Christ.'[13] The beatitudes give us an opportunity to learn how to do that in our generation, in the places and communities where God has placed us. Will you come with me on this journey to explore Matthew 5:1–16 – what St Chrysostom called a 'golden chain' – linked inseparably together in a way that will set us free to be the people God intended us to be? Welcome to the beatitudes.

This book can be used for personal study and reflection, and there are suggestions at the end of each chapter to help you do this. But it can also be used for discussion in a small group setting and there is a study guide at the end of each chapter too. I pray that, however you use it, it will be a blessing.

1

LIVING WITH GENUINE HUMILITY

Blessed are the poor in spirit, for theirs is the kingdom of heaven.
MATTHEW 5:3

The happiest people on earth

Who are the happiest people in the world? That is a question posed by the United Nations 'World Happiness Report' (March 2017),[14] following the first report published in April 2012. It aims to 'redefine the growth narrative to put people's well-being at the centre of governments' efforts'. The main six factors found to support happiness, it suggests, are: income, social support, health and life expectancy, freedom to make life choices, generosity and good governance (freedom from corruption). By these measurements, the report tells us, Finland was in first place in 2018, followed by Norway, Denmark, Iceland and Switzerland. The US has slipped to 18th place, five places down from 2016. The UK comes in 19th place (behind Germany, Canada and Australia) and many countries in Africa frequently appear towards the end of the list. In richer countries, the internal differences are not mainly explained by income inequality, but by differences in mental health, physical health and personal relationships. In poorer countries, income differences matter more, but, even there, mental illness is a major source of misery. Work is also a major factor affecting happiness. Unemployment causes a major fall in happiness, and even for those in work the quality of work can cause major variations in happiness.

These six criteria really matter and make a vast difference to people's lives; certainly, governments should be working at all of them. But each of them is founded on a set of values that are formed by a worldview, a set of beliefs about who we are, why the world exists and why it matters to be living happy and contented lives. Jesus would say that that worldview must have God at the centre of it, because he is the creator and sustainer of all life: 'In him we live and move and have our being' (Acts 17:28). So happiness – according to Jesus – flows from a worldview that has God at the centre. That is why each of the beatitudes begins with the exclamation 'Happy' or 'Blessed' – this is the deepest definition of happiness the world will ever know. This is the kind of life that brings true joy and from which flows a quality of life marked by these important criteria. This is what John Newton (1725–1807) expresses in that famous hymn, 'Glorious things of thee are spoken':

Solid joys and lasting treasure,
None but Zion's children know.[15]

Zion's children are people who have put God at the centre of their lives. They are happy and blessed in the ways that the beatitudes will describe. And the invitation is open to anyone: the sermon on the mount begins with Jesus teaching the disciples, but finishes with a large crowd listening in, amazed at his teaching. We too are invited to listen and learn to live in this way.

Poor in spirit

Let's be honest: we all love a bit of celebrity culture! It is incredibly hard to resist those alluring magazines at the hairdresser or the doctor's surgery, inviting us to nose around in the lives of the rich and famous.

There is a positive side to it all. Firstly, celebrity culture is mainly good for those who are being profiled because it gives them the status and publicity that usually help their careers and lifestyles. I say 'mainly good' because there is the downside of the paparazzi and public scrutiny, but that is the cost that comes with the fame. Secondly, it is good for the media industry because it is guaranteed to sell newspapers and magazines in their millions and attracts large audiences for TV chat shows. Thirdly, because celebrities are usually very successful in their professional and public life, by putting themselves 'out there' and becoming household names, they make us genuinely intrigued to know all about their personal lives as well: how are their relationships going, where did they go on holiday, who has had plastic surgery and what did they wear on their big night out at the Oscars? Fourthly, celebrities do a lot to promote good causes and support charitable initiatives – look at the phenomenal success of 'Band Aid' and 'Children in Need'.

There is, however, a darker, more worrying, downside to celebrity culture. It tends to divide the human race into two kinds of people: the famous and successful on the one hand, and the normal and mundane on the other, leaving most of the human race feeling insignificant, undervalued and unimportant. It encourages a voyeuristic curiosity and envy, causing us to aspire unrealistically to their luxurious lifestyles and vast fortunes. It allows some people to be fabulously wealthy when others have no food or home or access to healthcare. It leans towards an amoral assessment of human behaviour: because they are talented and famous, we make allowances for their excesses because that's what people like them do in their sphere of life owing to the pressures they are under. Worst of all, it feeds an overinflated view of their own importance, encouraging pride, superiority and misplaced self-satisfaction.

All of this seems a million miles from the first beatitude. The 'poor in spirit' are those who know the poverty of their own lives and their need of God to heal, forgive and restore. Davies and Allison explain the meaning like this:

In the Old Testament, especially in the Psalms, the Greek word and its Hebrew equivalents refer to those who are in special need of God's help... and in time 'poor' came to be a self-designation for the meek, humiliated and oppressed people of God.[16]

They have no delusions of grandeur, no pretentions to holiness, no inflated estimations of their own importance. Instead, they are desperately in need of God's saving help. They are not standing on an arrogant and misplaced self-confidence; instead, they are calling out to God for mercy and grace.

Jesus is also deliberately alluding to the great messianic prophecy in Isaiah 61:1: 'The Spirit of the Sovereign Lord is on me, because the Lord has anointed me to proclaim good news to the poor.' The 'poor in spirit' were, originally, the Jewish exiles suffering hardship and poverty in exile in Babylon. They had lost everything because of their own sin and disobedience to the requirements of the covenant: their land, their city, their temple, their status as the people of God, even their trust and confidence that God loved them and could rescue them. They were desperate, throwing themselves on the mercy and grace of God for help. So Jesus, by a deliberate reference to Isaiah 61:1, is declaring that this promise of salvation and blessing is now being fulfilled in an even more wonderful way. These people will know the restoration of their fortunes: 'for theirs is the kingdom of heaven' (Matthew 5:3).

In short, these people who are blessed have a humble spirit: they say with Isaiah: 'Woe to me... I am ruined! For I am a man of unclean lips, and I live among a people of unclean lips' (Isaiah 6:5). They pray with King David, after his adultery with Bathsheba and his murder of her husband, Uriah: 'For I know my transgressions, and my sin is always before me. Against you, you only, have I sinned and done what is evil in your sight' (Psalm 51:3–4). They say with the centurion, whose servant is desperately ill: 'Lord, I do not deserve to have you come under my roof. But just say the word, and my servant will be healed'

(Matthew 8:8). They exclaim with Peter, following Jesus' miraculous catch of fish: 'Go away from me, Lord; I am a sinful man' (Luke 5:8). They call out with blind Bartimaeus, sitting by the roadside, begging: 'Jesus, Son of David, have mercy on me!' (Mark 10:47). They say with Paul: 'Christ Jesus came into the world to save sinners – of whom I am the worst' (1 Timothy 1:15).

Jesus illustrated this spiritual poverty in the parable of the Pharisee and the tax collector (Luke 18:9–14). Two men went to the temple to pray. The Pharisee spent his time telling God how dutiful he had been in all his spiritual observances. The tax collector could not lift up his eyes to heaven, but beat his breast and said: 'God, have mercy on me, a sinner.' He was the one who went home justified, in a right relationship with God. He was poor in spirit, and the kingdom of heaven belonged to him.

This spiritual poverty is also seen in the parable of the lost son (Luke 15:11–31). The younger brother takes his share of the family inheritance and goes off to a far country, where he squanders it all on wild living. Poverty and hardship drive him back to his father's home: 'Father, I have sinned against heaven and against you. I am no longer worthy to be called your son; make me like one of your hired servants' (vv. 18–19). He has messed up big time and reached the end of his own resources. In his sheer desperation, he throws himself on the mercy and grace of his ever-loving father, and receives the most surprising and moving welcome:

> The father said to his servants, 'Quick! Bring the best robe and put it on him. Put a ring on his finger and sandals on his feet. Bring the fattened calf and kill it. Let's have a feast and celebrate. For this son of mine was dead and is alive again; he was lost and is found.' So they began to celebrate.
> LUKE 15:22–24

The poor in spirit are indeed blessed, for theirs is the kingdom of heaven.

Honesty and humility

The first beatitude, therefore, requires honesty and humility from us. Honesty is needed because it is not easy to admit that we are messed up and that we are fully responsible. More than that, we are caught in a trap that we can't escape from. We have reached the end of our resources and there appears to be no hope. This desperation is expressed in many hymns and prayers of God's people down the centuries, but perhaps nowhere more honestly and starkly than in 'Rock of Ages' by Revd Augustus Toplady (1740–78):

Nothing in my hand I bring,
simply to thy cross I cling;
naked, come to thee for dress;
helpless, look to thee for grace;
foul, I to the fountain fly;
wash me, Saviour, or I die![17]

What honesty to see ourselves as empty-handed, clinging on to the cross, naked, helpless, foul and soiled by our sin! This is what it means to be 'poor in spirit'. This does not deny that we are made in the image of God and therefore we are possessed of creativity and intelligence, of a capability for kindness and an ability to love. Nor does it deny the truth that we are infinitely precious in God's sight and known and loved by him to the very core of our being – for that is why he sent his Son to be our Saviour (John 3:16). But it is to be realistic and honest about the ways we have wounded that love and marred his image in us, as the Church of England prays in one of its prayers of confession.

Humility is the other requirement of the 'poor in spirit': there are no grounds for pride or arrogance for those who have to go, cap in hand, and ask for help. At university, I prided myself on being a fit and healthy young man who was used to getting a knock or two on the sports field. So when I got a squash ball hit into my eye during play, I shrugged it off as a black eye. A friend advised me to get it checked, so I reluctantly went up to the eye hospital. There they diagnosed a very serious eye injury that even threatened my sight, and I had to spend a week in hospital lying very still to allow it to recover. It was a humbling experience, but I am so glad I swallowed my pride and asked for help.

The 'poor in spirit' have done the same: they have swallowed their pride, admitted they need help and gone to find it from the healer of our souls, Jesus Christ. They have owned up to their sin, acknowledged their guilt and taken hold of the forgiveness that Christ has won on the cross. And because we continually stumble and fall, this becomes a lifelong attitude of mind: we return to the cross again and again in personal and public confession. Honesty admits we need help; humility enables us to go and find it.

I knew a man who told me that he never apologised to anyone about anything. The reason for this, he said, was that he was very intentional in everything he said and did, and took responsibility for his words and actions. He had no regrets and it would injure his pride and make him look small if he were to admit he had made a mistake and have to apologise. To a lesser extent, politicians fall into this way of thinking: they sometimes find it hard to admit that they made a mistake or said something wrong because it would be an admission of failure and so let their party down. Yet I believe the first beatitude allows us to admit our mistakes, own our failures and have the humility and courage to apologise and find forgiveness. I think the world needs people with honest humility, following the example of Jesus, who 'made himself nothing by taking the very nature of a servant… He humbled himself by becoming obedient to death – even death on a cross' (Philippians 2:7–8).

At Wimbledon in 2017, a new British star, Johanna Konta, was born in the hearts of the public, following a victory that won her a place in the Ladies Singles semi-finals against the legendary Venus Williams, an achievement that had not been seen on Centre Court for almost 40 years. Only two years earlier, she was labouring outside the top

150 seeds. 'Talented, dedicated, and growing fast into a national icon' was the headline in *The Times*. Yet she displayed a remarkable degree of humility for one who might, one day, become a Wimbledon champion. As she was leaving the court to the roar of the crowd, she stopped and made time to pose for a selfie requested by a Chelsea Pensioner; *The Times* said that he had grabbed 'the ultimate post-match selfie'. And in the interview afterwards, Konta said: 'In terms of the home support I feel very excited and very humbled by it'.[18]

If someone who is on the edge of stardom can display this level of genuine humility, how much more should those who profess to be followers of Christ? 'What does the Lord require of you? To act justly and to love mercy and to walk humbly with your God' (Micah 6:8).

Personal reflection[19]

Blessed are the poor in spirit, for theirs is the kingdom of heaven

- Am I poor in spirit, poor within, having abandoned everything to God?
- Am I free and detached from earthly goods?
- What does money mean to me?
- Do I seek to lead a sober and simple life that is fitting for someone who wants to bear witness to the gospel?
- Do I take to heart the problem of the terrible poverty that is not chosen by but imposed on so many millions of my brothers and sisters?

Prayerful response

Use Mary's song of praise (the Magnificat) as she is humbled and honoured to be the mother of the Messiah (Luke 1:46–55):

My soul glorifies the Lord
and my spirit rejoices in God my Saviour,
for he has been mindful
of the humble state of his servant.
From now on all generations will call me blessed,
for the Mighty One has done great things for me –
holy is his name.
His mercy extends to those who fear him,
from generation to generation.
He has performed mighty deeds with his arm;
he has scattered those who are proud in their inmost
thoughts.
He has brought down rulers from their thrones
but has lifted up the humble.
He has filled the hungry with good things
but has sent the rich away empty.
He has helped his servant Israel,
remembering to be merciful
to Abraham and his descendants for ever,
just as he promised our ancestors.

You could pray the following prayer:

Glory to the Father, and to the Son, and to the Holy Spirit, as it
was in the beginning, is now, and will be for ever. Amen

Discussion questions for small groups

Poor in Spirit

Starter (15 mins)
- Do you get dazzled by celebrity culture?
- What does contemporary society think will make people really
happy and contented?
- How much of this would Christians agree with?

Main course (60 mins)
- Put into your own words what Jesus meant by this opening beatitude.
- What kinds of people in the gospels illustrate this attitude of desperation for God's help?
- Describe a time when you have been desperate for God, and how he responded to your cries for help.
- Why is this attitude so countercultural in today's world?
- What is so attractive about people who are honest about their weaknesses and shortcomings, and are humble towards others?
- Who do you know who exemplifies this honesty and humility today?
- What steps could you take to 'humble yourself… under God's mighty hand' (1 Peter 5:6)?

Dessert (15 mins)
- Spend some time in open prayer, humbling yourselves before God.
- Let the Holy Spirit convict you of pride and arrogance, hardness of heart and an independent self-reliance.
- Silently confess any sins that are on your conscience, asking for God's forgiveness.
- Realise that we deserve nothing, but we are who we are because of God's grace and mercy.

2

LIVING WITH HEARTFELT SADNESS

Blessed are those who mourn, for they will be comforted.
MATTHEW 5:4

The earth is weeping

I am currently reading a fascinating book that tells the story of the Indian wars for the American West. The inside cover says: 'In a sweeping narrative, Peter Cozzens tells the gripping story of the wars that destroyed native ways of life as the American nation continued its expansion onto tribal lands.' It makes harrowing reading. The treatment of the Native Americans was 'an outrage', to use the words of one of the pre-eminent generals of the West, reflecting on the injustice of it all. 'When the Indians see their wives and children starving and their last source of supplies is cut off, they go to war. And then we are sent out to kill them. It is an outrage. All tribes tell the same story.'[20] One missionary, describing the feelings of the Indians as they were constantly driven out of land that they had previously inhabited, said: 'The very earth seems sliding from beneath their feet.'[21] A young Miniconjou warrior called Dewey Beard described one of the massacres of Indians known as the Wounded Knee Ravine tragedy – this time of women, children and elders – when a Hotchkiss gun shelled the area where the terrified non-combatants were hiding: 'And then there went up from [my] dying people, a medley of death songs that would make the hardest hearts weep.'[22]

It is right that we should weep with them over what happened. Yet this is just one example among many of 'man's inhumanity to man'. Our history books are full of the most devastating acts of barbarity, cruelty and exploitation, many of the worst of them happening in the lifetimes of our parents and grandparents. My uncle was in a Japanese POW camp in Burma and survivors have told us of the bitter hardships that had to be endured. The Holocaust, with the systematic extermination of Jews, gypsies, mentally handicapped, homosexuals, etc., was undoubtedly the darkest period of human history. Numbers range from eleven to seventeen million killed in all Nazi genocides and war crimes, with 6 million Jews executed in the concentration camps.

The Rwandan genocide of 1994 killed up to one million people, which was approximately 20% of Rwanda's population and 70% of the Tutsi people: 75,000 surviving children were orphaned. Bosnian Serb forces in 1995 killed more than 8,000 Bosnian Muslims at Srebrenica and Žepa; wider ethnic cleansing during the 1992–95 Bosnian War involved the expulsion of another 25–30,000 Bosniak civilians. The genocide of Yazidis by ISIL from 2014 to the present has been numbered in the thousands. The earth is still weeping.

Added to these are tragedies of poverty and starvation. Oxfam and other relief agencies are warning us as I write that millions of men, women and children are in need of urgent help in South Sudan, Somalia, Ethiopia and Kenya. Natural disasters also take a heavy toll of human life in some of the poorest communities of the world: Haiti is the poorest country in the Americas and the country with the highest number of deaths caused by disasters in the past two decades, most of them occurring during the catastrophic earthquake of 2010 with 222,570 fatalities. The Boxing Day tsunami in 2004 in the Indian Ocean, caused by a mega earthquake, affected 14 other countries but Indonesia's death toll was the highest – 130,736 of the 165,708 fatalities. Cyclone Nargis hit Myanmar in 2008 and resulted in 138,000 deaths. The earth is still weeping.

There is also deep sadness over our environmental crisis. Experts tell us that climate change, due to pollution of the atmosphere by greenhouse gases, has observable ecological and social effects. The depletion of ozone in the stratosphere results in increased levels of harmful solar ultraviolet (UV-B) radiation reaching the earth's surface, causing a range of health-related and ecological problems. Worldwide, approximately one billion people live in industrial cities where unhealthy levels of air pollution occur; and water quality is seriously degraded by contamination with pollutants, giving rise to a range of health-related and ecological effects (such as the degradation of coral reefs). Land contamination has occurred as a result of chemical and radioactive pollution, and around half of the world's mature forests have been cleared by humans despite their being an essential part of the global ecosystem and of the biosphere. They help to regulate climate; they protect soils from erosion; and they provide habitats for a vast number of plant and animal species. In 1999, the United Nations Environment Programme (UNEP) estimated that one quarter of the world's mammal species and around one tenth of the world's bird species faced a significant risk of total extinction. The earth is still weeping.

Blessed are those who mourn

We have noted that Bible scholars who have written commentaries on the beatitudes identify Isaiah 61:1–7 as the key Old Testament passage that Jesus is deliberately alluding to. This is a messianic passage that announces hope for the Israelites who are languishing in exile in Babylon, torn away from their land, their city and their temple. Davies and Allison again: 'Mourning is heard because the righteous suffer, because the wicked prosper, and because God has not yet acted to reverse the situation.'[23]

> By the rivers of Babylon we sat and wept when we remembered Zion.
> PSALM 137:1

Yet this will all change when the Messiah comes, says the prophet Isaiah. He will revive the fortunes of the nation, and restore Israel to her promised land. Consequently, their mourning will turn into joy: 'He has sent me to… comfort all who mourn… to bestow on them a crown of beauty instead of ashes, the oil of joy instead of mourning and a garment of praise instead of a spirit of despair,' (Isaiah 61:1–3). Craig Evans also points us to Jeremiah 31:13 ('I will turn their mourning into gladness; I will give them comfort') because 'this verse is part of a larger complex of oracles in Jeremiah 31 that speak of Israel's redemption, restoration and covenant renewal'.[24]

These Old Testament passages help us to understand the second beatitude: 'Blessed are those who mourn, for they shall be comforted' (Matthew 5:4). Jesus is clearly identifying himself as the Messiah who has come to announce an end to the mourning of exile: not just the exile of being separated from the land and city and temple, because that had already happened for the Jewish nation, but an end to the estrangement from God, and the rebuilding of the kingdom of heaven on earth. Those who long for this, and who grieve over the pain and brokenness of the world in its separation from God, will be comforted by the arrival of the messianic kingdom, the renewal of the covenant and the making of all things new, when God 'will wipe every tear from their eyes. There will be no more death, or mourning or crying or pain' (Revelation 21:4).

A time to weep

There is an understandable tendency in our culture today to try to blot out the sad and painful realities of our world. Media coverage brings us so close to terrible tragedies and there is a very real anxiety of overexposure to human suffering. We can't take it any more! We want to run away and hide like ostriches, burying our heads in the sand. We want exotic holidays that transport us into another world of luxurious hotels and beautiful places. We attempt to drown our sorrows with alcohol or deaden the pain with recreational drugs. We try to escape to nice, comfortable districts that shelter us from the challenges of urban poverty. We rush past the homeless person on the street who is asking for help. We escape into our safe, private worlds of social media, romantic novels and DVD box sets.

Now we need to keep a balance here. I am not suggesting that Christians should be killjoys, unable to enjoy themselves and the many good things in the world that God has given us. Holidays, social media and the delights of food and drink can all be enjoyed in sensible moderation, and it is important to keep a work/life balance, to make time for our friends and family and not to get overexposed to and wearied by the world's pain. Our human flourishing allows us to be happy and contented people who treasure all that God has given us to enjoy with thanksgiving and delight.

But none of this should be seen as an escape from the hard edges of life. The earth is still weeping and it is appropriate that we should share that pain and weep too. There is a place for tears as well as joy in the Christian life. The people of God in both Old and New Testaments have modelled this for us. The psalmist said, 'Streams of tears flow from my eyes, for your law is not obeyed' (Psalm 119:136). Jeremiah, thought to be the author of the book of Lamentations, described the pain of exile: 'My eyes fail from weeping, I am in torment within; my heart is poured out on the ground, because my people are destroyed' (Lamentations 2:11). Nehemiah wept on hearing that the walls of Jerusalem were still in ruins and his people were vulnerable to attack: 'For some days I mourned and fasted and prayed before the God of heaven' (Nehemiah 1:4).

In the New Testament, Jesus wept over impenitent Jerusalem, which would not receive him as her Messiah (Luke 19:41). Paul wept over churches that were being troubled by false teachers who 'live as enemies of the cross of Christ' (Philippians 3:18). John, on the island of Patmos, broke his heart when, in his vision of heaven, no one was initially found to open the scroll in the right hand of God and so unfold his purposes for his people: 'I wept and wept because no one was found who was worthy to open the scroll or look inside' (Revelation 5:4). The good news that the elder brought him must have come as a tremendous relief (v. 5), for the Lion of Judah is worthy, who turns out to be 'the Lamb who was slain' (v. 6).

Christians down the centuries have continued to weep over the brokenness of the world and the sin in their own lives. It has frequently been the starting place for revivals. The 18th-century evangelist Jonathan Edwards, even though he was very reasoned and measured in his preaching, frequently wept in prayer over the sinners of his day, seeing thousands touched by the love of Christ as he preached the gospel. David Brainerd, a missionary to Native Americans, wrote:

> God enabled me to so agonise in prayer that I was quite wet with perspiration… the Lord visited me marvellously in prayer. I think my soul never was in such an agony before. I felt no restraint, for the treasures of divine grace were opened to me. I wrestled for my friends, for the ingathering of souls, for multitudes of poor souls.[25]

Robert Murray M'Cheyne, the minister of St Peter's Church in Dundee, knew the importance of weeping. He not only spent hours in prayer, crying over his people, but cried over them in the pulpit. 'The secret of M'Cheyne's ministry was that he carried the burden of his people, of his nation and of God's cause upon his heart'.[26] The evangelist Charles Finney wrote of a time when he wrestled with God over a great problem he was facing. He speaks of being 'loaded down with great agony… I struggled and groaned and agonised, but could not manage to present my case before God in words, but only in groans and tears. The Spirit struggled within me with groanings that could not be uttered.'[27]

I personally found myself deeply moved as I read the harrowing story of a North Korean girl, Yeonmi Park.[28] After her father was sent to a labour camp for black-market trading, her family faced starvation.

She managed to escape with her mother to China in 2007 but fell into the hands of human sex traffickers before eventually escaping to Mongolia with the help of Christian missionaries. Moving to South Korea in 2009, she is now a human rights activist, advocating for victims of human trafficking in China. I was stunned by her courage and moved to tears in almost every chapter. I found myself praying: 'Lord, have mercy!'

Moira Stuart, an unflappable former BBC newsreader, took part in a BBC2 documentary in March 2007 in which she explored William Wilberforce's part in ending Britain's shameful slave trade.[29] Her ancestors included both a slave and a slave owner. During her visit to Ghana, she was taken on a tour of Cape Coast Castle by Dr Abena Busia, a Ghanaian writer and academic, and was shown cells where prisoners starved or suffocated to death. When she saw boats on the adjacent beach, where slaves were led by British merchants to be exchanged for sugar, cotton and rum, she was overwhelmed. She broke down in tears and was unable to speak.

Do we allow ourselves to be moved by the pain of the world? On the website of the Christian magazine *Relevant*, there is an excellent article by Drew Griffiths, written in July 2016, following a spate of public tragedies including the horrific shooting in Orlando and massive terrorist attack in Istanbul, Turkey. It is entitled 'Christians have to mourn injustice':

> Scarcely a day passes when we're not confronted with unspeakable tragedy accompanied by unrelenting grief. We never have the chance to mourn fully, to recover our emotional health before we are plunged again into the mourning cycle… Christians occupy a special place in this conversation. We are called to mourn over the presence of sin in our lives – and in the world around us… Our challenge is… to mourn well.[30]

To 'mourn well', he suggests, involves *sympathy*, having a broken heart for others in their pain and loss; *empathy*, feeling the emotions alongside them; *self-criticism*, seeing the darkness and sin in our own lives; and *hope*, knowing we have a Saviour who overcomes evil with good.

So where are the tears of God's people? They are precious to God, as the Israelites discovered when they cried out to him in their bitter hardship and slavery in Egypt (Exodus 2:23–25). In fact, says the psalmist, these tears of lament are so special to him that he stores them up in a bottle (Psalm 56:8, NRSV). The rector of St Aldates, Oxford, Canon Charlie Cleverly, writes in 'Rule of life', based on the beatitudes:

> When God works, it seems there is often the mourning that Jesus calls 'blessed' – mourning over sin, deep regret for being away from God, longing for 'home' and the hope of a homecoming to God. All this leads to tears… people cry over loved ones who are away from God, they cry for children and young people and the elderly, and over the general state of society.[31]

Personal reflection

Blessed are those who mourn, for they shall be comforted

- Do I consider affliction a misfortune and a punishment, as some people in the world do, or as an opportunity to be like Christ?
- What are the reasons when I am sad: the same as God's or the same as the world's?
- Do I seek to console others or only to be consoled myself?
- Do I know how to keep an adversity a secret between God and me, not talking about it every chance I get?

Prayerful response

A prayer of Archbishop Thomas Cranmer as the Collect for Lent

Almighty and everlasting God,
you hate nothing that you have made
and forgive the sins of all those who are penitent:
create and make in us new and contrite hearts
that we, worthily lamenting our sins
and acknowledging our wretchedness,
may receive from you, the God of all mercy,
perfect remission and forgiveness;
through Jesus Christ your Son our Lord,
who is alive and reigns with you,
in the unity of the Holy Spirit,
one God, now and for ever. Amen[32]

Discussion questions for small groups

Those who mourn

Starter (15 mins)
- When did you last cry?
- Do tears come easily to you?
- Are they a sign of weakness?

Main course (60 mins)
- Why were the Israelites mourning in exile in Babylon (Psalm 137:1), and how was their comfort going to come (Isaiah 40:1)?
- In what ways do we experience similar feelings of being in exile today, causing us to mourn like the Israelites?
- Do you feel a godly grief over persistent sins in your own life? Do you find it a help to take that grief to the Lord in confession and repentance?

- What situations in the world do you finding yourselves grieving over? Why do they matter to you and how do you channel your grief?
- Try to describe how God feels about these situations. How do we know that his heart breaks over his broken and hurting world?
- How does God comfort us in our mourning and bind up the broken-hearted? Can you give an example of how he has done that for you?

Dessert (15 mins)
- Take a while to remember how God feels about our sins, and what it cost him to pay for our forgiveness (Mark 10:45). Spend some time asking for forgiveness.
- Remember situations in the world where there is terrible suffering and over which God's heart must break: lift them before the Lord and cry to him for him to intervene and bring comfort.
- Praise God that there will be an end to crying and pain and tears, and ask him to usher in a kingdom where all sin and suffering will be banished (Revelation 21:1–4).

3

LIVING WITH GENTLE STRENGTH

Blessed are the meek, for they will inherit the earth.
MATTHEW 5:5

Bullies and bullets

There was a fascinating letter in *The Guardian* on 6 July 2017, written by the Principal of the College of Haringey, Enfield and North East London, responding to a letter criticising the lack of democratic accountability of those who form housing policy in the UK. He begins his letter by completely agreeing with this sentiment:

Chairman Mao famously said, 'All power comes out of the barrel of a gun.' A bit blunt, perhaps, but essentially true. Power is essentially about forcing others to do what you want. Power bullies, power pushes opposition aside. In modern societies, as Antonio Gramsci argued, governments try to get their way through consent – by getting the majority to agree with their viewpoint. But in the end, consent is all too often backed up by coercion. The baton and the bullet usually trump the ballot box.[33]

This was the same week that tensions were rising between North Korea and the USA over Pyongyang's successful intercontinental ballistic missile testing. The North Korean news had reported President Kim Jong-un 'feasting his eyes' on the missile and showed him breaking into a broad smile, complete with footage of him punching the air and hugging delirious generals. But many thought that Trump's response, talk of 'sending an armada to the Korean peninsula or bombing North Korea', simply played into the stereotype of Americans propagated by the North Korean media, and compounded the political tension. All this seems to confirm the truth that the world is at the mercy of the power bullies and that 'all power comes out of the barrel of a gun'. And there is a sad truth here for those who choose to believe it and live by it.

But in the third beatitude, Jesus offers us a better and nobler truth: 'Blessed are the meek, for they will inherit the earth.' At first sight, it might look as if Jesus has lost the plot! Surely the losers can't be the winners? John Stott expresses the apparent disconnect:

> One would have expected the opposite. One would think that meek people go nowhere because everyone ignores them or rides roughshod over them and tramples them underfoot. It is the tough, the overbearing who succeed in the struggle for existence: weaklings go to the wall.[34]

The meek shall inherit

There is, however, on closer examination, a deeper wisdom here. The Greek adjective *praus* means 'gentle', 'humble', 'considerate', and this reminds us of how Jesus defined himself: 'I am gentle [*praus*] and humble in heart' (Matthew 11:29). Paul also describes Christ as having 'humility and gentleness' (2 Corinthians 10:1). One commentator sets the meaning of this beatitude in the wider context of the two previous beatitudes, where we recognise that we are 'poor in spirit' and 'those who mourn':

> Meekness is essentially a true view of oneself, in expressing itself in attitude and conduct to others... the man who is truly meek is the one who is truly amazed that God and man can

think of him as well as they do and treat him as well as they do.[35]

Dr John Stott concludes: 'This makes him (or her) gentle, humble, sensitive, patient in all his dealings with others.'[36]

The key Old Testament background is, firstly, Psalm 37, where 'the wicked plot against the righteous' (v. 12), who are also referred to as the 'poor and needy' (v. 14). But 'the evil men' do not triumph in the end, for God has the last word, for the day of judgement is coming (v. 13). In the light of this reversal of fortunes, 'the meek will inherit the land and enjoy peace and prosperity' (v. 11). The original meaning of 'the land' would have had a more literal sense of 'the promised land', which had been promised to Abraham, the father of the Israelite nation (Genesis 13:14–17). Here, Jesus widens the meaning into a spiritual inheritance of the heavenly kingdom, as R.T. France explains: 'There is a general tendency in the New Testament to treat the Old Testament promises about "the land" as finding fulfilment in non-territorial ways, and such an orientation seems required here.'[37]

The other Old Testament passage behind the third beatitude is, again, Isaiah 61:1–7. Here, the poor and the mourning inherit 'a double portion in [their] land, and everlasting joy will be [theirs]' (v. 7). Jesus is making another eschatological claim about the new messianic kingdom that is being inaugurated in his own life and ministry: the Messiah will bring a reversal of fortunes. It is not the proud, arrogant bullies who 'win' in the end, who have the last laugh, and who achieve world dominion. Rather, it is the meek and the humble followers of the Messiah, those whom the world thinks are insignificant nothings and nobodies, who inherit all that God has for them. This is ultimately fulfilled in the new heaven and earth that God is preparing for the end of time (Revelation 21:1–4), but there is a present and partial fulfilment now, in this life, when we begin to enjoy the treasures of the kingdom of heaven and the privileges of being sons and daughters of our heavenly Father. This is our 'double portion' and 'everlasting joy' (Isaiah 61:7).

This reversal of fortunes that Jesus promises is a reason for quietly trusting in God and waiting for his deliverance (Psalm 37:1–8). We mourn and grieve over the world's sin and brokenness (as Matthew 5:4 says), but we don't despair. We don't lose heart and become cynical about the way things are going. We don't cave in to a pessimistic fatalism that 'nothing is ever going to change'. On the contrary, everything is going to change. The world will be put to rights, and everything will be made new. The 'winners' become the 'losers', and the 'losers' become the 'winners'. The meek will inherit the earth!

Max Hastings, in his book *All Hell Let Loose: The world at war 1939–1945*, vividly describes the trauma of Pearl Harbor, when the Japanese sank the American navy in a surprise attack on 7 December 1941. One of the US sailors who survived the attack described what he saw the next day:

> We were flabbergasted by the devastation… The water was covered with oil, fires were burning still, ships were resting on the bottom mud, superstructures had broken and fallen… For sailors who had considered these massive ships invincible, it was a sight to be seen but not comprehended. We seemed to be mourners at a spectacular funeral.[38]

The Japanese went on to achieve a number of victories in South East Asia in what Hastings calls 'a season of triumph'. However, all this was to change, as he describes in his next chapter, entitled 'Swings of fortune'. He concludes: 'Within a year of Pearl Harbor, the arrest of Japan's Asian and Pacific advances, and the beginning of their reversal, made its doom inevitable.'[39]

What an incredible reversal of fortune! But nothing compared to the reversal of fortune that God has brought about through our Lord Jesus Christ, who promises that the meek shall inherit the earth. This has been accomplished and sealed through the Messiah's death and resurrection. A painting called *Checkmate*, by the artist Moritz

Retzsch, used to be displayed at the Louvre Museum in Paris but is now in private ownership, after being sold at Christie's in 1999. It shows two chess players, one being Satan (who appears arrogantly confident) and the other a man who looks sad and resigned and trapped because, if this is checkmate, then Satan wins and he gets the man's soul. The story goes that a chess champion once visited the museum and, after studying the painting for quite a while, suddenly announced: 'It's wrong! The painting tells a lie! The king has one more move!' He had noticed that the arrangement of the chess pieces was incorrect. The man, who thought he was losing, was winning, because his king had one more move left, which would make him the winner of the game.

And this is the story of Easter: Satan truly believed that he had Jesus nailed when he watched him die on the cross in humiliating pain and spiritual torment. 'My God, my God why have you forsaken me'? (Matthew 27:46). He's powerless to save himself. This whole messiah thing has gone tragically wrong… Checkmate! But wait a minute – or wait three days, to be precise! The King has one more move and his resurrection is not just a narrow escape from the jaws of defeat, to fight another day; it is the decisive move that wins the battle, defeats his enemy and ushers in God's redemptive purposes for the world. And, more than that, we (who are joined to Christ) share in that victory, becoming inheritors of the kingdom of God and one day reigning with him in glory. All seemed to be lost, but the King had one more move!

Gentle strength

This 'reversal of fortune' makes sense of the third beatitude and shows us how it can be true that 'the meek shall inherit the earth'. In the light of this, we can live differently, displaying a gentle strength in all our dealings with others. I have the privilege of being the chaplain in the oldest surviving academic institution in Oxford named after a medieval saint, St Edmund, who had a distinguished career in the early 13th century (Oxford academic, parish priest, cathedral canon and Archbishop of Canterbury in the reign of Henry III), but with a humble spirit and a servant heart. His spirituality, character and integrity not only had a profound influence on his contemporaries, but continue to inspire individuals and institutions today, 900 years later.

I think it is the meekness of St Edmund that has impressed me the most. For example, while teaching at Oxford, he was known to be exceptionally kind to his students. Cecil Plaxton has given us a wonderful description of this in his *Treasure of Salisbury*:

> In Oxford, the students lived in Inns and Halls enduring all sorts of hardships that they might pursue the art of learning. The great bell of St Mary's Church would call them to attend their lectures. At midday, there would be disputations. In the evenings pupils would meet their tutors to discuss the day's learning. Edmund, meditative as ever, gentle and unworldly, took no payment from his poorer pupils. He never counted their fees to save them from embarrassment. He watched over them with paternal care. He sat up all night with one who was sick and dying.[40]

His humble spirit is seen also at the time of his appointment as archbishop in 1233. This was one of the most senior positions in the English medieval hierarchy of legislative power. Plaxton reminds us:

> By long tradition, the archbishop of Canterbury was the foremost councillor of the realm and the spiritual director of the king... The title 'Primate of all England' gave him the moral authority to act as a spokesman for the whole English Church.[41]

Edmund always retained that humble attitude before God, even when he was offered this most prestigious position in the Church of England. When envoys from Canterbury came to tell him the news of his election as archbishop, he shed 'profuse tears and heaved deep sighs', protesting that he was unfit, humbling himself in these words: 'I am a worm, and no man. I have neither the merit nor the learning which you suppose. All the world is deceived in this respect.'[42] It was only after he was persuaded by the Bishop and Chapter at Salisbury that he at last reluctantly accepted it, for fear that the Pope might appoint a foreign prelate instead. He concluded: '[God], who knows all things, knows that I would never consent to this election unless I thought that I would sin mortally by refusing it.'[43]

His gentleness and sensitivity are also seen in his dealings with family after the death of their mother. He personally settled his young, unmarried sisters, Margaret and Alice, into a quiet and safe nunnery at Catesby and constantly watched over their welfare. In a touching personal gesture of tenderness before he died, he bequeathed his grey cloak to his sister Alice, who 'felt the cold' at Catesby.[44] When Archbishop of Canterbury, he welcomed a lady from Catesby because she was a friend of his sisters. He also was a great pastoral help to Ela, Countess of Salisbury, when her husband died and supported her in her plans to set up Lacock Abbey, where she eventually became the abbess.

To people like St Edmund, the meek, Jesus promises that they shall 'inherit the earth', which seems very ironic considering it is usually the powerful and self-assertive who seem to get what they want and leave their mark. Yet there is a very real sense in which the ground that Edmund inhabited (Abingdon, Oxford, Paris, Salisbury, Calne, Canterbury and Pontigny) bears his footprint and continues to hold his presence: in stone statues, in stained glass, in historic buildings, in sacred writings and, most of all, in the hearts and minds of those who value his legacy.

Mother Teresa's ministry to the starving and destitute in Calcutta during the second half of the 20th century, responding to God's call to serve him in the faces of the poor, required great meekness and humility. She is therefore well placed to help us to understand the countercultural nature of this quality:

> Humility is the mother of all virtues… It is in being humble that our love becomes real, devoted and ardent. If you are humble, nothing will touch you, neither praise nor disgrace, because you know what you are. If you are blamed, you will not be discouraged. If they call you a saint, you will not put yourself on a pedestal.[45]

This is an important corrective at a time when churches are thinking hard about enabling church growth, emphasising 'inspiring leadership', 'transforming communities', 'powerful ministries' and 'successful programmes'. Attention is often taken by the megachurches and televangelists rather than the smaller, more modest churches in inner-city and rural areas. We must be careful not to lose sight of the upside-down values of the messianic kingdom: the servant king, gentle and humble in heart, washed his disciples' feet before taking his place on the throne of heaven; the self-giving lamb, who was slain for us, is now vindicated, exalted and heir of all things and invites us to reign with him. *The meek* shall inherit the earth.

Personal reflection

Blessed are the meek, for they shall inherit the earth

- Am I meek?
- Accepting that there is not only violence of action but also violence of speech and thought, do I control anger outside of and within me?
- Am I kind and friendly to those around me?

Prayerful response

A prayer by Mother Teresa of Calcutta:

> Dear Lord, the Great Healer, I kneel before you,
> since every perfect gift must come from you.
> I pray, give skill to my hands,
> clear vision to my mind,
> kindness and meekness to my heart.
> Give me singleness of purpose,
> strength to lift up a part of the burden
> of my suffering fellow men,
> and a true realisation of the privilege that is mine.
> Take from my heart all the guile and worldliness
> that with the simple faith of a child,
> I may rely on you.
> Amen[46]

Discussion questions for small groups

The meek

Starter (15 mins)
- What do you think of the current world leaders and their leadership styles?
- Who do you most and least admire?

Main course (60 mins)
- Surely everyone knows that 'power comes from the barrel of a gun', and that it is the rich and powerful, the brash and the bullies, who get what they want? So are you tempted to think that this beatitude is nonsense?
- How were Jesus' meekness and gentleness expressed (Matthew 11:29)? In what sense were his life and ministry a 'reversal of fortune'?

- How does having a realistic view of oneself lead us towards meekness?
- Who do you know who has genuine meekness and humility, and how does it show itself in them?
- In what sense do the meek inherit the earth? Is this a present reality or a future hope?
- 1 Peter 5:6 tells us to humble ourselves under the mighty hand of God; how do we do this and what difference will it make?

Dessert (15 mins)

- Take some time to meditate on the meekness of Christ, submitting to the will of God for his life, submitting to the authority of scripture, and above all submitting to the humiliation of the cross. Praise the servant king, the lamb who was led to the slaughter.
- Confess the pride and arrogant self-confidence that love being the centre of attention and believe that we have a right to be noticed, to be heard and to get our own way.
- Ask the Lord to humble you, to give you the meekness of Christ, and to enable you to be a servant of others without being noticed.

4

LIVING WITH DRIVING PASSION

Blessed are those who hunger and thirst for righteousness, for they will be filled.

MATTHEW 5:6

Fine dining

As I get older, I find myself genuinely enjoying the finer things of life. This week I went with my son on a tour of the Fuller's Brewery at Chiswick, and loved learning about the brewing process and sampling the results! Last summer, on a trip to Cape Town, Ruth and I went on a tour of the vineyards of Stellenbosch and sampled some of the most delicious South African wines. In relation to food, I have developed a love of international cuisine, and was delighted to be treated on my birthday by my family to a mouth-watering curry in Veeraswamy, England's oldest and most famous Indian restaurant, in Regent Street, honoured in the Michelin Guide of 2017. Formal dinners at St Edmund Hall, where I work as a chaplain, are always a treat too!

Food and drink are a big feature of modern Western culture, and fine dining and fine wines are seen by many as the ultimate experience of fine living. Programmes about cooking, including the ones that add in an element of competition (*MasterChef* and *The Great British Bake Off*, for example), are watched by millions, ourselves included. Alcohol is used as one of the primary ways to relax after a busy day at work or at weekends, and binge drinking is still a major public order problem for the police in towns and city centres across Europe. Fast-food outlets are always heaving with young people, but there is increasing alarm about the long-term health implications of what some would call 'junk food'.

So, again, all this suggests a need for a healthy balance. On the one hand, we should appreciate the richness and variety of God's good creation (Genesis 1:26–30) and receive with thanksgiving God's good gifts, enjoying the fruits of the harvest (Psalm 65:9–13; 67:6–7). Harvest festivals under both old and new covenants are the expressed annual opportunity to recognise God's generosity. Delicious food and fine wines are gifts to be enjoyed, and God has declared all food 'clean' (Acts 10:9–15; Romans 14:14). Yet we should note that the same passage in Romans has a cautionary word about wrong attitudes to food and drink – and note the mention of 'righteousness': 'For the kingdom of God is not a matter of eating and drinking, but of righteousness, peace and joy in the Holy Spirit' (v. 17). So if fine dining becomes the high point of our lives, we have simply missed the point! The inhabitants of Jerusalem in Isaiah 22 had made this mistake when the prophet warned of invasion and called the people to weeping and repentance. They flippantly replied: 'Let us eat and drink… for tomorrow we die' and indulged in joyful revelry, with the eating of meat and the drinking of wine (v. 13).

Worse than that, there is a sin of gluttony, which one dictionary defines as 'a limitless appetite for food and drink and overindulgence to the point where one is no longer eating just to live, but rather living to eat',[47] which we can recognise in many Western cultures. This is not the only thing Paul is talking about in Philippians 3 when he is describing 'enemies of the cross of Christ', but it certainly includes people who are gluttons: 'Their destiny is destruction, their god is their stomach and their glory is in their shame. Their mind is set on earthly things' (v. 19).

Another important reason for balance and restraint, which should speak to Christians with sensitive consciences, is the world's poor: the Food and Agriculture Organization of the United Nations estimates that about 795 million people of the 7.3 billion people in the world, or one in nine, were suffering from chronic undernourishment in 2014–2016.[48] Almost all the hungry people, 780 million, live in developing countries, representing 12.9 per cent, or one in eight, of the population of developing countries, with 11 million people undernourished in developed countries. This causes godly restraint and compassion, ensuring that we are not only mindful of the millions who go to bed hungry every night, but that we pray for them and do what we can to alleviate their suffering, motivated by the love of Christ himself. Otherwise, 1 John 3:17 ('If anyone has material possessions and sees a brother or sister in need but has no pity on them, how can the love of God be in that person?') becomes a description of us and asks questions about the reality of our Christian faith.

So is there an alternative – something that is more noble and satisfying for us to desire as the driving passion of our lives? Jesus offers us the answer in the fourth beatitude: 'Blessed are those who hunger and thirst for righteousness, for they will be filled' (Matthew 5:6).

Personal and public righteousness

'Righteousness' is one of those magnificent Bible words that means different things in different contexts, so it is important to understand the setting in order to tease open the meaning of any usage. When speaking about God, it is a description of his perfect holiness, faithfulness and justice: 'The Lord is righteous in all his ways and faithful in all he does' (Psalm 145:17). When referring to God's people, the 'righteous' are those who have been made 'right with God' through the free gift of salvation, received by faith in God's Messiah, Jesus Christ (Romans 1:17; 3:21–26; 2 Corinthians 5:21). Jesus would have had both of these meanings in mind when he used the word in the fourth beatitude.

But 'righteousness' can also mean the forming of a righteous character through the sanctifying work of the Spirit. This has to be in Jesus' mind because the rest of the sermon on the mount will give many examples of a deeper righteousness of the heart, over against the public and superficial righteousness of the Pharisees on the one hand (Matthew 5:20; 6:1), and the unrighteous and ungodly behaviour of the gentiles/pagans on the other (Matthew 5:47; 6:7, 32). Jesus' examples cover many practical aspects of Christian living: angry and lustful thoughts, marital unfaithfulness and divorce, prayer and fasting, justice and forgiveness, giving and generosity, attitude to money and possessions, and so on. In all of these ways, we must 'seek first the kingdom of God and *his righteousness*' (Matthew 6:33, my italics). The followers of Jesus are to be different from the outwardly religious and the openly pagan by reflecting the beauty and holiness of their heavenly Father (Matthew 5:48). 'Blessed are those who hunger and thirst for righteousness' means pursuing this kind of godly character and life, in the way that Jesus did: 'My food... is to do the will of him who sent me and to finish his work' (John 4:34).

And yet 'righteousness' also includes the aspect of 'putting the world to rights' in the way that God intended, vindicating God's name among the nations: 'The Lord has made his salvation known and revealed his righteousness to the nations' (Psalm 98:2). This must also have been in Jesus' mind because, as we have seen, Isaiah 61 forms the backdrop to the beatitudes. In Isaiah 61:3, the exiles who are poor, broken-hearted and mourning in captivity are longing for vindication: the throwing off of ungodly rule and the establishment of God's justice. They will be comforted with joy and gladness and become 'oaks of righteousness, a planting of the Lord, for the display of his splendour'. Those who hunger and thirst for this have a driving passion for God and his ways – nothing matters more than restoring the honour and glory of God in the communities and nations where they live. Therefore, pursuing righteousness is all about longing for the vindication of God's name and God's people on earth: 'Your kingdom come, your will be done, on earth as it is in heaven' (Matthew 6:10), as Jesus taught us to pray.

God's servants are to hunger and thirst for the restoring of the honour of God in all the earth, so that he is known and loved and human life is conformed to his will. This naturally involves a social righteousness, whereby Christ's followers must work towards freedom from oppression, injustice, discrimination and poverty, in line with the ministry of the Messiah in Isaiah 61:1–3. This is not an 'add-on' to the church's mission; this is an integral aspect of the messianic kingdom because God is redeeming the whole world. Nothing is outside the scope of this redeeming work: schools, prisons, banks, shops, councils, parliament, law firms, leisure centres, hotels, homeless centres, builders' firms, hospitals, pubs, the internet and social media – all are places where we are to hunger and thirst for righteousness, and where we will be seeking first the kingdom of God and his righteousness (Matthew 6:33).

Jesus is calling his people to hunger and thirst for personal *and* public righteousness. In fact, it wouldn't be appropriate for us to have one without the other. If we hungered for change in our world but neglected to allow that change to take place in our own lives, we could be accused of double standards and hypocrisy. But if we longed for a personal righteousness but ignored the social and political outworking of the gospel in the communities and places where we live, we could be rightly accused of an irrelevant and self-indulgent piety. So our calling is to hold these two aspects of Christian discipleship together: pursuing the glory of God in both our private lives and the public square.

Hungry and thirsty for God's glory

The Christian MP William Wilberforce and his small group of Christian activists and social reformers, known as the Clapham Sect because they all met at Holy Trinity Church, Clapham Common, are a good example of people who had hunger and thirst for righteousness, in both their personal and public lives. They engaged together in a range of social causes for the transforming of 19th-century British society, including prison reform, prevention of cruel sports, the alleviation of poverty, illiteracy and child abuse, and the suspension of the game laws and the lottery. They also supported several mission and Bible societies, financed Hannah More's schools and pamphlets, and published their own journal, *The Christian Observer*.

But their greatest achievement was their leadership of the campaign to abolish slavery. In 1814, they managed to get one tenth of the population to sign anti-slavery petitions, which were delivered to the House of Commons. In 1818, Wilberforce wrote in his diary: 'In the scripture, no national crime is condemned so frequently and few so strongly as oppression and cruelty, and the not using our best endeavours to deliver our fellow-creatures from them.'[49] He needed resilience as well as passion, because anti-slavery bills were defeated in Parliament for eleven consecutive years before the act abolishing the slave trade was passed in 1807. The second reading of the Emancipation Act, bringing slavery to an end in the British Empire, was passed in 1833, and Wilberforce died three days later. The 19th-century historian W.E.H. Lecky said: 'The unweary, unostentatious, and inglorious crusade of England against slavery may probably be regarded as among the three or four perfectly virtuous pages comprised in the history of nations.'[50]

In 1865 William and Catherine Booth, the founders of the Salvation Army, began their ministry to the poor and destitute of London's East End, bringing the good news of Jesus Christ to alcoholics, criminals and prostitutes. Their aim was to combine evangelism and social welfare to change the social landscape of England by eradicating poverty and lifting the urban poor out of moral decay, through setting up hostels for the homeless and ex-prisoners and farming communities where they could learn basic agricultural skills. Booth also provided a range of professional resources for the poor, including lawyers, clinics, schools and banks. He believed that if the state was failing to meet its social obligations then Christians must step up. He was a fighter for spiritual and social righteousness:

While women weep, as they do now, I'll fight. While little children go hungry, as they do now, I'll fight. While men go to prison, in and out, in and out, as they do now, I'll fight. While there is a drunkard left, while there is a poor lost girl upon the streets, while there remains one dark soul without the light of God, I'll fight – I'll fight to the very end![51]

And he did. He died in 1912 and, in response to public demand, his body lay in state at Clapton and 150,000 people came to pay their respects to 'the world's best-loved man', whom the Mayor of South Shields described as 'the archbishop of the world'. 35,000 people attended his memorial service in August 1912, includ§ing Queen Alexandra and representatives of King George V and Queen Mary. The funeral took place the next day and the city of London stood still for nearly four hours; Bramwell Booth, who gave the address at the graveside, said: 'If you were to ask me, I think I could say that the happiest man I ever knew was the General. He was a glad spirit. He rose up on the crest of the stormy billows, and praised God, and laughed at the Devil's rage, and went on with his work with joy.'[52]

Jesus had promised this: 'Blessed [happy] are those who hunger and thirst for righteousness, for they will be filled' (Matthew 5:6). William Booth's legacy was a movement that serves the world's poorest communities in 58 countries.

Among the many excellent Christian organisations that continue this tradition of social activism today (CAFOD, Christian Aid, Tearfund, Compassion, World Vision, etc.), let me mention CARE (Christian Action, Research and Education) as an example of one that works for a fairer and godlier society, pursuing righteousness in the way that Jesus invited us to do in the fourth beatitude. Their aims are to equip individuals and local churches for prayer and action, to have an impact in the political world, to provide research and briefings for parliamentarians, to train Christian graduates through a leadership programme and to support the vulnerable through advocacy. I am always struck by the range of vital causes they support and pray about. In their prayer diaries, we are invited to pray for the millions of victims of human trafficking and agencies that support them; those caught up in domestic violence and addictive patterns of behaviour; children and young people who are affected by poverty; challenges faced by rural and farming communities; older and dependent people and those who care for them; the negotiations over Britain's exit from the European Union; schools, teachers and pupils; the millions caught up in conflicts and wars; the use of technology, robotics, social media and the internet; issues relating to abortion and euthanasia; and the political uncertainty in Scotland, Wales and Northern Ireland. Wilberforce would have been proud of them!

Professor N.T. Wright, previously Bishop of Durham, encourages us in this in his book *Surprised by Hope*, which explains the meaning of the resurrection of Christ for the whole world and the church's mission. He draws our attention to 1 Corinthians 15:58, the conclusion of the great chapter on the resurrection of the body, and suggests that the final verse comes as a surprise. It doesn't say, 'Sit back, relax, chill; your future hope is secure and heaven awaits you', as we might expect. It says, 'Therefore, my dear brothers and sisters, stand firm. Let nothing move you. Always give yourselves fully to the work of the Lord, because you know that your labour in the Lord is not in vain.' Doesn't it seem strange that our *future* hope results in *present* service for the glory of God: what's the point if the Lord is coming back and there will be a new heaven and earth? Paul's answer is because 'our labour is not in vain'. N.T. Wright writes:

> What you do with your body in the present matters… Painting, preaching, singing, sewing, praying, teaching, building hospitals, digging wells, campaigning for justice, writing poems, caring for the needy, loving your neighbour as yourself – all these things will last into God's future. They are not simply ways of making the present life… a little more bearable, until the day when we leave it behind altogether… They are part of what we may call 'building for God's Kingdom'.[53]

Do you have a hunger and thirst for God's glory and honour? Are you seeking first the kingdom of God and his righteousness? Will you fight for social and spiritual transformation? If so, then Jesus promises satisfaction for the whole of eternity, when 'the earth will be filled with the knowledge of the glory of the Lord as the waters cover the sea' (Habakkuk 2:14). Can anything be more satisfying than this?

Personal reflection

Blessed are those who hunger and thirst for righteousness, for they shall be satisfied

- Do I hunger and thirst for holiness, or am I at times satisfied with mediocrity and lukewarmness?
- Does the physical hunger of millions of people lead me to question my continual search for comfort or my middle-class lifestyle?
- Do I realise how much I and the world in which I live resemble the rich man who feasted daily?

Prayerful response

A fourfold Franciscan blessing[54]

May God bless you with a restless discomfort about easy answers, half-truths and superficial relationships, so that you may seek truth boldly and love deep within your heart.

May God bless you with holy anger at injustice, oppression, and exploitation of people, so that you may tirelessly work for justice, freedom and peace among all people.

May God bless you with the gift of tears to shed with those who suffer from pain, rejection, starvation or the loss of all that they cherish, so that you may reach out your hand to comfort them and transform their pain into joy.

May God bless you with enough foolishness to believe that you really can make a difference in this world, so that you are able, with God's grace, to do what others claim cannot be done.

And the blessing of God the supreme majesty and our Creator, Jesus Christ the incarnate Word who is our brother and Saviour, and the Holy Spirit, our advocate and guide, be with you and remain with you, this day and for evermore. Amen

Discussion questions for small groups

Hungering and thirsting for righteousness

Starter (15 mins)
- When were you last really hungry and thirsty?
- What did it feel like and how did it focus the mind?
- What did it feel like to finally have a good meal?

Main course (60 mins)
- What do you find yourself chasing after in life? Are you drawn towards the pleasures of luxurious living and fine dining? Are these appetites wrong and displeasing to God?
- Put into your own words what you think Jesus meant by this 'hungering and thirsting for righteousness'. How does this relate to Matthew 6:33?
- Is personal holiness something that you seek after and pursue, as Paul encourages Timothy in 1 Timothy 6:11? How might you increase your appetite to grow in your spiritual life? Is this your work or the Spirit's work (Colossians 1:28–29; 2 Corinthians 3:17–18; Ephesians 5:15–18)?
- Can you share an example of where you have pursued an issue of social righteousness?

- Were you fulfilled in this service, filled with joy and wonder at what God was doing through you? Did you see change and blessing?
- Which figures in church history inspire you to pursue social change in the name of Christ, and why?

Dessert (15 mins)

- Invite the Lord to search you and try you, as requested by the psalmist in Psalm 139:23.
- Ask the Lord to increase your desire to be holy, like Christ.
- Commit to God those areas of social injustice that God has put on your heart.

5

LIVING WITH
HEALING GRACE

Blessed are the merciful, for they will be shown mercy.
MATTHEW 5:7

Obsessed with revenge

It would not be an exaggeration to say that modern culture is obsessed with the theme of revenge. True, it has always been there, as Homer's *Iliad* illustrates with its multiple revenge motif: the core of the story is Menelaus seeking revenge against Paris for stealing his wife, Helen, along with Achilles hunting Hector down for killing Patroclus. Shakespeare used the revenge narrative in a number of his plays: in *Hamlet* it is those who are remedying a perceived wrong, in *Othello* betrayal is the motive, and in *The Merchant of Venice* it is harmed feelings. Dumas' *The Count of Monte Cristo* explores the revenge of Edmond Dantès on the people responsible for his false imprisonment and has inspired no fewer than 30 films and television series. Victor Hugo's *Les Misérables* has as its central theme the story of Jean Valjean being pursued by the vengeful Javert for petty infractions of the law, and the West End musical has broken box office records, as has the film. The thriller writer John Grisham has employed vengeance as one of his main motifs, including the revenge reaction to the rape of a daughter and domestic. Agatha Christie's murder mysteries between 1920 and 1976 often employ revenge as the main motive for the killing. Modern fiction uses the revenge motif too, so the recent thriller *Nomad* by James Swallow invites us into the world of MI6 and counter-espionage against the backdrop of jihadists taking revenge on a corrupt Western civilisation that has exploited them and their people. In the book, the briefing at a terrorist training camp for Arab teenage orphans in a Middle Eastern desert is as follows:

> The nations of our enemies, our oppressors... the Americans, the Europeans, the Russians... these are the ones who have hurt us... A man with courage and spirit, who can look beyond fear, cannot be stopped. He may take his revenge wherever he finds it.[55]

Yet it is the modern film industry that most clearly reveals this obsession. The 2015 *Video Hound Guide to Films* lists more than a thousand films under the heading of 'Revenge', making it the largest category, indicating that this is a major theme permeating popular culture. The kind of actions that provoke revenge are physical attacks on the victim or a member of their family, bullying, and sexual violence and hurt feelings by someone ending a relationship. A classic case of this latter motif of revenge is the spurned mistress in the film *Fatal Attraction* (1987), where Glenn Close, the film's villainous star, is jilted by Michael Douglas, her lover, and stalks him and his family.

One of the most popular versions of the revenge motif in films during the last 50 years has been the vigilante film based around offences against family or friends that avoid detection by the justice system – but where the offended knows who did the crime. Having lost respect for the police, the law and the justice system, they take matters into their own hands. As one of the vigilante film posters put it: 'What do you do when justice fails?'[56] Martin McDonagh's double-Oscar-winning film, *Three Billboards Outside Ebbing, Missouri* is a classic example of the popularity of this genre; it tells the story of a plucky vigilante who confronts both the police and the tragedy of her daughter's death by erecting roadside monuments to her grief and rage.

These films and books that celebrate revenge and glamorise the avengers as heroes are hugely popular and gripping, but they help to shape a mindset that fosters angry thoughts, harbours grudges and legitimises personal revenge. Honour killings are an extreme version of this way of thinking: a member of a family is killed by a spouse or relative because it is believed that the victim has brought shame or dishonour upon the family, or has violated the principles of a community or a religion in one of many ways. But TV programmes such as *Neighbours from Hell* and *The Nightmare Next Door* show real-life stories of unresolved and bitter conflicts between neighbours, providing voyeuristic entertainment. Yet we all know what it is to have fallen out with someone, to bear grudges and resentments over a perceived offence or hurt, to be angry with 'the system' for not protecting us or resolving our grievance. A complaint and compensation culture is now commonplace because this is what we do with our frustration and anger. Is there a better way?

Loving justice and mercy

The Bible celebrates and upholds justice as a foundational principle that governs the universe. God is everywhere spoken of as a just judge (Genesis 18:25; Psalm 75:7; Revelation 20:11–15) and he loves justice and abhors evil and wrongdoing (Isaiah 61:8; Psalm 33:5; Romans 12:19). It is important to note that God's justice in the Bible is not seen as in tension with or a contradiction of his love, but as an *expression* of it: because he is a loving God, he will bring justice for the oppressed and the abused, and uphold the cause of his people because of his covenantal, steadfast love. And, to add to his desire for justice, he has put rulers and judges in place to execute justice, punish offenders and uphold the cause of the oppressed (Exodus 18:13–27; Isaiah 1:17; Romans 13:1–5). All of this is an anticipation of the end time when God will judge the world in righteousness on a day that he has fixed, when the Lord returns, and all will be called to give an account of their lives (Acts 17:31; Revelation 20:11–12).

Isaiah 61, which we have seen is the key Old Testament text in the mind of Jesus as he gives the beatitudes, is written in the wider context of God's *having mercy* on the Jewish exiles, even though the exile itself was a punishment from God for the disobedience of his people:

Comfort, comfort my people,
    says your God.
Speak tenderly to Jerusalem,
    and proclaim to her
that her hard service has been completed,
    that her sin has been paid for,
that she has received from the Lord's hand
    double for all her sins.
ISAIAH 40:1–2

Now, when the Messiah comes, there will be instead a double portion of *blessing*, which explains why every beatitude begins with that word:

Instead of your shame,
    you will receive a double portion,
and instead of disgrace,
    you will rejoice in your inheritance.
And so you will inherit a double portion in your land,
    and everlasting joy will be yours…
All who see them will acknowledge
    that they are a people the Lord has *blessed*.
ISAIAH 61:7, 9, my italics

The wonder of the gospel, then, is that God, the just judge, also loves mercy. In fact, he is called 'the Father of mercies' (2 Corinthians 1:3, NRSV) and he is 'rich in mercy' (Ephesians 2:4). The context of 'rich in mercy' is that all of humankind have followed the way of the world and become objects of divine wrath (Ephesians 2:3). Knowing this helps us to appreciate the riches of God's mercy: 'But because of his great love for us, God, who is rich in mercy, made us alive with Christ even when we were dead in transgressions – it is by grace you have been saved' (Ephesians 2:4–5). In other words, he delights to show his mercy towards us, offered through our Lord Jesus Christ, even when we don't deserve it in the slightest (Romans 3:21–26; 5:6–8).

The 'merciful' in the fifth beatitude, then, are those who have understood and experienced the undeserved mercy of God. We have all wandered from God's ways, we have lived as though he didn't exist and we have ignored the overtures of his love towards us. Despite this wanton rebellion, God pursued us in the person of his Son, allowing him to die on the cross that we could be forgiven and brought back into relationship with God. As Charles Wesley expressed it in his famous hymn 'And can it be': 'Tis mercy all, immense and free; for, O my God, it found out me.'[57]

This means that we now must be merciful to others: those who oppress us, those who exploit others, and those who are exploited – the poor, the vulnerable, people on the edges of society. We experience God's mercy in order to show mercy to others, including our enemies. We should note how 'mercy' is a big theme in Matthew's gospel. Parables will often illustrate what it means to be merciful: the parable of the sheep and the goats calls Christ's followers to show mercy, kindness and practical help to the most vulnerable members of the community (Matthew 25:31–46), and the parable of the unmerciful servant illustrates how hypocritical it is to receive mercy from God, but not to act mercifully towards others (Matthew 18:21–35). We must be merciful to our enemies, not just our friends (Luke 6:35–36) and Jesus taught us to pray, 'Forgive us our debts, as we also have forgiven our debtors' (Matthew 6:12). Jesus uses Hosea 6:6 on two occasions ('I desire mercy, not sacrifice') to expose the hypocrisy of the Pharisees who seem to abide by all the covenantal requirements of God's law, but ignore the most important duty to show kindness and compassion to people (Matthew 9:13; 12:7). Two blind men call out to Jesus, 'Have mercy on us, Son of David', and he does (Matthew 9:27), restoring their sight, which is all the more significant when Isaiah 61:1 says that the Messiah will proclaim 'release from darkness for the prisoners', which the Septuagint translates 'recovery of sight to the blind'. This is the mercy of God.

Easier said than done

I suspect that this beatitude is one of the easiest to agree with, and yet the hardest to put into practice. Of course, most people want to live in a world where people love their enemies, are able to 'forgive and forget', and where the weak and vulnerable are shown kindness and compassion. But when we are wronged, or insulted, or abused, or pushed aside by an employer, or denied justice by the system, our feelings of anger, bitterness, resentment and hatred easily surface, fuelled by a compensation and revenge culture. Forgiveness, mercy and compassion are lofty ideals but pragmatically impossible. Didn't Jesus give vent to his anger in the temple courts with the money changers, turning over their tables and calling it 'a den of robbers' (Luke 19:46)? Yes, he did, but his angry actions were not fuelled by thoughts of personal revenge or hatred, but by a zeal for the right use of his Father's house and anger at the exploitation of worshippers coming to the temple to offer their sacrifices. This cleansing of the temple was about justice and compassion for the worshippers, and the honour and glory of God. The tables had to be turned.

A better place to see Jesus exemplifying the fifth beatitude is on the cross. Jesus has been falsely accused, wrongly sentenced, physically scourged, humiliatingly stripped, cruelly mocked, emotionally deserted and roughly impaled – but he avoids thoughts of hatred and revenge, and he utters no angry insults. Instead, he prays for his executioners: 'Father, forgive them, for they do not know what they are doing' (Luke 23:34). A little while later, Stephen is called to be the first Christian to give his life in his service of the Lord and he similarly prays for mercy on his executioners (Acts 7:60). Since then, there has been a noble line of martyrs, saints and disciples who have experienced wrongs, abuses and injustices but shown mercy and forgiveness towards their oppressors.

St Edmund of Abingdon, archbishop and saint in the reign of Henry III, is, again, an outstanding medieval example of someone who was merciful. He showed mercy as a teacher in Oxford to poor students who could not pay their fees, demanding no payment. He showed mercy to the poorest members of the community when at Salisbury, according to the testimony of Stephen the sub-dean at the cathedral: 'He refused hospitality to none. To the poor and sick he was bountiful and compassionate, for which cause he was always burdened with debt.'[58]

Robert the Cistercian added:

Of his works of mercy... the shelter of his roof was open to every wayfarer, and no one who asked for alms went away from his door empty-handed. In time of famine, he caused to be bestowed on all, with generous compassion, bread, pulse, herbs.[59]

A final example of his merciful spirit was his kindness towards his enemies, those who had made life so difficult for him, particularly as archbishop. He forgave the Chapter at Canterbury, who had caused him such heartache, in one of his last letters before he died, and he also was long-suffering with the King who often dealt harshly with him: 'He implored the king, with all humility, with faithfulness, and with all meekness.'[60]

More recently, three remarkable examples of a merciful spirit stand out in my mind. The first is Corrie ten Boom, a Dutch Christian who, along with her sister Betsie and their father, was sent to the Nazi concentration camp at Ravensbrück during World War II for hiding Jews. Her sister and father died there but Corrie was released, owing to a 'clerical error'. After the war, in 1947, she returned to Germany with the message that God forgives. During her talk, she suddenly noticed that one of her prison guards, who had been exceptionally cruel, was sitting in front of her. He came up to her afterwards and thrust out his hand as an appeal for forgiveness. Her own hand froze in her notebook as memories of harsh lights, sharp ribs, piles of dresses and naked shame came flooding back to her. She knew Jesus' words: 'If you do not forgive men their trespasses, neither will your Father in heaven forgive you', so she prayed silently: 'Jesus, help me!' Mechanically, she thrust out her hand into the one stretched out to her. She then describes what happened:

> And as I did, an incredible thing took place. The current started in my shoulder, raced down my arm, sprang into our joined hands. And then this healing warmth seemed to flood my whole being, bringing tears to my eyes. 'I forgive you, brother,' I cried, 'with all my heart!' For a long moment we grasped each other's hands, the former guard and the former prisoner. I had never known God's love so intensely, as I did then. But even then, I realised it was not my love. I had tried, and did not have the power. It was the power of the Holy Spirit.[61]

My second example is Gordon Wilson, a Northern Irish Christian, who had been attending a peaceful Remembrance Day service in Enniskillen, Northern Ireland with his daughter Marie in 1987, when an IRA terrorist bomb went off. He held his daughter's hand as they lay trapped beneath a mountain of rubble. The rescuers dug them out of the rubble and rushed them to hospital, but she and nine other people died.

William Ury wrote in his 1999 book *The Third Side*:

> In an interview with the BBC, Wilson described with anguish his last conversation with his daughter and his feelings toward her killers: 'She held my hand tightly, and gripped me as hard as she could. She said, "Daddy, I love you very much." Those were her exact words to me, and those were the last words I ever heard her say.' To the astonishment of listeners, Wilson went on to add, 'But I bear no ill will. I bear no grudge. Dirty sort of talk is not going to bring her back to life. She was a great wee lassie. She loved her profession. She was a pet. She's dead. She's in heaven and we shall meet again. I will pray for

these men tonight and every night.' As historian Jonathan Bardon recounts, 'No words in more than 25 years of violence in Northern Ireland had such a powerful, emotional impact.'[62]

Wilson subsequently became a campaigner for peace in Northern Ireland, meeting with the Provisional IRA and loyalist paramilitaries to urge them to abandon violence. Gerry Adams, the leader of Sinn Féin, offered a formal apology on Remembrance Day 1997 for the Enniskillen bombing.

The third inspiring example of exceptional mercy is the foot washing of prisoners by Pope Francis at the traditional Holy Week Mass and Washing of the Feet. In 2013, during the first Holy Week of his pontificate, he celebrated this in the juvenile prison of Casal del Marmo, choosing to wash the feet of twelve inmates, including a Muslim woman. In 2015, he held this ceremony again in the prison of Rebbibia, washing the feet of six men and six women. One of the inmates, an African woman with tears in her eyes, held her child on her lap and the Pope washed the child's feet. In April 2017, he did it again, washing the feet of twelve prisoners at the Italian prison of Paliano. Among them were three women and a Muslim, who was baptised as a Christian a few months later, and two of the prisoners were serving life sentences. Although some might think that this symbolic gesture is a religious stunt to catch the eye of the media, those who know him see it as a totally genuine act of mercy, consistent with his former practice when he was Archbishop of Buenos Aires, and with character and beliefs in line with the Lord Jesus' own act of self-humbling and compassion in the upper room with his twelve apostles on the night before he died (John 13). His first Vatican-authorised book, detailing his vision for the Catholic Church, is appropriately entitled *The Church of Mercy* (Loyola Press, 2014), where Pope Francis calls the church to move beyond its own walls to bring God's mercy wherever suffering, division or injustice exists.

Although, as we noted earlier, Shakespeare deals with themes of vengeance in his plays, he does so to celebrate mercy as the chief

Christian virtue. The best example of this is in *The Merchant of Venice*, Act IV, Scene 1, set in a Venetian court of justice. The speech is made by Portia, disguised as Balthazar, a young lawyer, who pleads with Shylock for mercy; it is widely regarded as one of Shakespeare's greatest speeches, presenting mercy as an invaluable quality for the most powerful and influential people in society:

> The quality of mercy is not strain'd,
> It droppeth as the gentle rain from heaven
> Upon the place beneath: it is twice blest;
> It blesseth him that gives and him that takes:
> 'Tis mightiest in the mightiest: it becomes
> The throned monarch better than his crown…
> It is enthroned in the hearts of kings,
> It is an attribute to God himself;
> And earthly power doth then show likest God's
> When mercy seasons justice.[63]

Where does this 'gentle rain from heaven' need to fall today (Matthew 5:38–47)? On the European migrant community as they flee war zones and famine areas; on our overcrowded and understaffed prisons; on the homeless community of our cities and towns; on sex offenders, hard-right facists and jihadist terrorists; on those who have wounded and hurt us? Those who are merciful will receive mercy themselves (Matthew 5:7), not because they deserve it or have earned it, but because they have shown themselves to be children of the 'Father of mercies'.

Personal reflection

Blessed are the merciful, for they will be shown mercy

- Am I merciful? When a brother, a sister or a coworker demonstrates a fault, do I react with judgement or with mercy?

- Jesus felt compassion for the crowds; do I?
- Have I, at times, been the servant who was forgiven but does not forgive others?
- How many times have I casually asked for and received the mercy of God for my sins without taking into account the price that Christ paid for me to receive it?

Prayerful response

Pope Francis composed a special prayer for the Jubilee Year of Mercy (December 2015–November 2016). In the prayer, he entreats the Lord to make the Jubilee of Mercy a year of grace so that the church, 'with renewed enthusiasm, may bring good news to the poor, proclaim liberty to captives and the oppressed, and restore sight to the blind'. Note the references to Isaiah 61:1–3 here, which was the key Old Testament text in Jesus' mind as he spoke the beatitudes.

Lord Jesus Christ, you have taught us to be merciful like the heavenly Father, and have told us that whoever sees you sees him. Show us your face and we will be saved. Your loving gaze freed Zacchaeus and Matthew from being enslaved by money; the adulteress and Magdalene from seeking happiness only in created things; made Peter weep after his betrayal, and assured Paradise to the repentant thief... You are the visible face of the invisible Father, of the God who manifests his power above all by forgiveness and mercy.

Let the church be your visible face in the world... Send your Spirit and consecrate every one of us with its anointing, so that the Jubilee of Mercy may be a year of grace from the Lord, and your church, with renewed enthusiasm, may bring good news to the poor, proclaim liberty to captives and the oppressed, and restore sight to the blind. We ask this through... you who live and reign with the Father and the Holy Spirit for ever and ever. Amen[64]

Discussion questions for small groups

Showing mercy

Starter (15 mins)
- What are your favourite films?
- How many of them have a revenge motif?
- Why are they so appealing?

Main course (60 mins)
- Share your experience of coming to Christ and receiving mercy from God – how has it changed you?
- How are God's justice and God's mercy held together in the Bible? Can you give examples?
- How do you react when someone wrongs you or hurts you? Is it inappropriate to want some kind of justice, or should we always forgive?
- Do you feel merciful to any particular vulnerable people groups: those caught up in poverty, or sex-trafficking, or migrants, or prisoners, or the homeless?
- Have you been inspired by someone's ministry of mercy? If so, who and why?
- Why is this beatitude so countercultural?

Dessert (15 mins)
- Begin by praising God for the mercy he has shown to us in Christ, and thank him for the cross by which our forgiveness is possible.
- Pray for a merciful spirit towards others, particularly those who have wronged us or hurt us.
- Ask the Lord to give you opportunities to show mercy towards the weak and vulnerable in our society: the migrants, the homeless, the prisoners, those with mental health issues, those with learning disabilities, and more.

6

LIVING WITH
HOLY INTEGRITY

Blessed are the pure in heart, for they will see God.
MATTHEW 5:8

Double standards

Does personal integrity matter any more? Do our private lives need to match up to our public and professional responsibilities? Is strength of moral character still viewed as an asset in a job application? Do parents need to apply the same standards of behaviour to themselves that they expect from their children? Can a teacher be disciplined for viewing pornography, if discovered? Should there be a public outcry over politicians who fiddle their tax forms and expenses claims? Should priests be allowed to continue in public ministry if they have committed a sexual offence? Should a celebrity be blacklisted for dressing up in a Nazi uniform for a fancy-dress party? Should somebody with a gambling addiction be employed by a bank?

The answers to these questions are not as obvious as they might have been 70 years ago. Life is, arguably, more complex now and definitions of acceptable personal behaviour have changed, along with a public/private split that allows people to have a large measure of moral freedom in private (apart from criminal activity) as long as it doesn't affect their public and professional performance. After all, the argument runs, none of us is perfect so we need to make allowances for private misdemeanours and character flaws. Didn't Jesus say: 'Let any one of you who is without sin be the first to throw a stone' (John 8:7), so the real hypocrites are those who pass judgement on others? Isn't that exactly what Jesus taught in the saying: 'First take the plank out of your own eye, and then you will see clearly to remove the speck from your brother's' (Matthew 7:5)? We should have expectations of high moral standards in our public and professional lives, but what we do in private is our own business. A priest said recently in a group discussion that I was in: 'Why would God be interested in what goes on in the bedroom?' People nodded in warm agreement.

This popular position has a point. It is true that we are all fallen and there is no perfection this side of heaven, even for archbishops and popes. It is true that we come into our public life and professional roles with character traits and personality weaknesses. It is true that Jesus strongly condemned a judgemental spirit that could see the faults in others but missed the huge shortcomings in our own lives. But if this position stops there and consequently promotes 'keeping up appearances' in public while allowing for a large measure of personal moral laxity in private, then we may have redefined integrity to mean exactly the opposite of what the word actually means!

All the dictionary definitions I have seen go beyond defining integrity as a personal quality of someone who has strong moral principles; they include the idea of being whole, complete or undivided. When this is applied to a person, it suggests an integration of values so that there is no separation between belief and practice, between public and private. Integrity is therefore the opposite of hypocrisy, which can be defined as either the inconsistency of saying or believing one thing and doing another, or doing something noble for the wrong motive (e.g. to impress others).

> The word 'integrity' evolved from the Latin adjective, *integer*, meaning whole or complete. In this context, integrity is the

inner sense of 'wholeness' deriving from qualities such as honesty and consistency of character. As such, one may judge that others 'have integrity' to the extent that they act according to the values, beliefs and principles they claim to hold.[65]

Amy Rees Anderson, the managing partner of REES Capital and the founder of the IPOP Foundation, a charity focused on educating entrepreneurs, writes on the Forbes website and reflects on the urgent need for integrity in the entrepreneurial world of business and enterprise:

> We live in a world where integrity isn't talked about nearly enough... 'The end justifies the means' has become an acceptable school of thought for far too many. Sales people overpromise and underdeliver, all in the name of making their quota for the month. Applicants exaggerate in job interviews because they desperately need a job. CEOs overstate their projected earnings because they don't want the board of directors to replace them. Entrepreneurs overstate their pro formas because they want the highest valuation possible from an investor. Investors understate a company's value in order to negotiate a lower valuation in a deal. Customer service representatives cover up a mistake they made because they are afraid the client will leave them. Employees call in 'sick' because they don't have any more paid time off... In each case the person committing the act of dishonesty told themselves they had a perfectly valid reason why the end result justified their lack of integrity.

She sums up:

> If I could teach only one value to live by, it would be this: success will come and go, but integrity is forever. Integrity means doing the right thing at all times and in all circumstances, whether or not anyone is watching. It takes having the courage to do the right thing, no matter what the consequences will be.[66]

It appears that integrity matters after all, and Jesus would wholeheartedly agree.

Pure in heart

The sixth beatitude is not a call to perfection, but to integrity at the deepest level. The commentators unanimously agree that the root meaning of 'pure in heart' is a total consistency between belief and practice, between 'life' and 'lips', between heart and mind. There is no 'double-mindedness' or 'double standards'. The pure in heart are consistent, integrated, whole people, with the added dimension of living solely for the glory of God. This is spelled out very clearly, for example, by Davies and Allison in their commentary on this beatitude:

> Purity of heart must involve integrity, a correspondence between outward action and inward thought, a lack of duplicity, singleness of intention and the desire to please God above all else… to will one thing, God's will, with all of one's being.[67]

So our love for God should not just be expressed only in public acts of worship but is to be woven into the very fabric of daily life. Jesus will go on to make this point very forcibly in the rest of the sermon, emphasising purity of the eye in the way we look at the opposite sex (Matthew 5:27-28), purity of motive in acts of generosity (6:2-4), praying (6:5-8) and fasting (6:16-18) and purity of heart in our willingness to forgive (5:38-47). Jesus was the only person who has shown total consistency in every area of his life, but we are called to be like him as people who claim to follow him.

The key Old Testament passage that Jesus is thinking of in this beatitude is likely to be Psalm 24:3-6. In answer to the question 'Who may ascend the mountain of the Lord?', referring to the spiritual requirement for pilgrims arriving at Jerusalem to worship, the answer comes:

The one who has clean hands and a pure heart,
   who does not trust in an idol,
   or swear by a false god.
They will receive blessing from the Lord…
Such is the generation of those who seek him,
   who seek your face, God of Jacob.

PSALM 24:4–6

There is an emphasis on inward purity here, whereby truthfulness, a clean conscience and a genuine seeking after God are the requirements for God's blessing in gatherings for corporate worship. This has a particular relevance to the Judaism of Jesus' day, which laid a great stress on ritual purity: to be 'pure in heart' implies a contrast with the meticulous observance of outward, ceremonial purity. True religion is a purity of the heart.

Added to this is the setting of Isaiah 61:1, where the broken-hearted now receive their healing, purity of heart and wholeness, in the day of the Messiah, the divine physician who will 'arise with healing in his wings' (Malachi 4:2, KJV).

Psalm 24:6 ('those who seek [God's] face') is now fulfilled with a vision of God: 'They shall see God' (Matthew 5:8). There are wonderful moments of epiphany in both Old and New Testaments (Exodus 24:9–10; Isaiah 6:1; Matthew 17:1–8; John 2:11; Revelation 1:12–17),[68] and Jesus may well have been encouraging his disciples with promises of more to come. Yet commentators are clear that the primary focus of Jesus' promise is eschatological: a privilege of those who are called to the New Jerusalem (Revelation 22:4; 1 Corinthians 13:12; 1 John 3:2).

Here on earth the people of God may find strength 'as if seeing the one who is invisible' (Hebrews 11:27), but such 'seeing' remains only a foretaste of the true vision of God in heaven.[69]

Guard your heart!

When the word 'heart' is used in a conversation, it could mean one of 43 definitions, according to one dictionary: the vital organ that pumps blood round the body, the symbol of romantic love, the epicentre of a city or a community, a passionate feeling about a cause, the quality associated with courage, and so on. It is a rich and variable word, and one must listen very carefully to the context in order to understand how it is being used at any given time.

However, none of these definitions do justice to the biblical concept of the heart: the main meaning of the word in the Bible is altogether richer and fuller than any of these individual ones. In Hebrew thought, human beings were a totality: not 'a body plus a soul', but a living unit of vital power – of which the heart was the epicentre. Our personality, character, feelings and intellect altogether are nearer to the biblical concept of the heart. The heart expresses the real 'me'. It is the location of my spiritual, emotional, moral and mental DNA. One Bible dictionary defines it:

> The centre or focus of our inner personal life. The heart is the source, or spring, of motives, the seat of the passions, the centre of the thought processes; the spring of conscience. Heart (in the Bible) is associated with what is now meant by the cognitive, affective and volitional elements of personal life.[70]

Understood like this, it seems obvious that the heart is the most important part of us. Proverbs 4:23 makes this point very powerfully: 'Above all else, guard your heart, for everything you do flows from it.' That is very countercultural in today's world: billions of pounds are spent each year on an advertising industry that says: 'If we want to be good, cool people, we need the latest smartphone, or to wear the latest outfit, or to drive the new convertible car. This is what really matters, and this is what will make you a person that others will respect and want to know.'

But the Bible says: 'This isn't true!' These are not bad things in themselves, but not what really matters, and it is certainly not wise to spend our lives pursuing them. 'Above all else, guard your heart, for everything you do flows from it.' What really matters is not the outward, but the inward; not the appearance, but the substance; not the trappings of life, but the heart. Who we are (at the very centre of our being) matters a lot more than how we express ourselves. And when we pay attention to that, almost without trying, we win people's respect and they want to hang around us.

I'm learning this at St Edmund Hall, Oxford, where I am a University Chaplain and Co-Senior Welfare Officer. I don't think God requires me to be the most dynamic chaplain they have ever had, going to every sporting event and hanging out in the college bar until 3.00 in the morning! He is asking me to be a person of integrity who pays attention to my heart, and who is therefore able to minister to others from a depth of character, and so help strengthen the life of the community.

Integrity matters in how we speak and our ability to speak the truth. One of the worrying features of our time is the concept of 'post-truth', which the 2016 Oxford Dictionaries declared as their 'international word of the year'. It is defined as an adjective that describes the use of emotion and personal interpretation as more important in persuading public opinion than objective facts. Editors said that use of the term had increased by around 2,000 per cent in 2016 from the previous year and was largely due to 'the context of the EU referendum in the United Kingdom and the presidential election in the United States'.[71] The Oxford Dictionaries' President, Casper Grathwohl, said:

> We first saw the frequency really spike this year in June with buzz over the Brexit vote and Donald Trump securing the Republican presidential nomination. Given that usage of the term hasn't shown any signs of slowing down, I wouldn't be surprised if post-truth becomes one of the defining words of our time.[72]

In contrast to this cultural trend, a disciple of Jesus is called to be 'pure in heart', allowing our speech to be transparently truthful and unexaggerated, telling the truth as it is without any attempts to 'cover things up' or 'present in its best light'. Using oaths or promises should not be necessary, because our words can be trusted without any need to bolster confidence in them with 'I promise':

> Again, you have heard that it was said to the people long ago, 'Do not break your oath, but fulfil to the Lord the vows you have made.' But I tell you, do not swear an oath at all: either by heaven, for it is God's throne; or by the earth, for it is his footstool; or by Jerusalem, for it is the city of the Great King. And do not swear by your head, for you cannot make even one hair white or black. All you need to say is simply 'Yes' or 'No'; anything beyond this comes from the evil one.
> MATTHEW 5:33–37

Christian worship that has integrity and brings joy to God is also a matter of the heart. Paul writes to the church at Ephesus and says:

> Do not get drunk on wine, which leads to debauchery. Instead, be filled with the Spirit, speaking to one another with psalms, hymns, and songs from the Spirit. Sing and make music from your heart to the Lord, always giving thanks to God the Father for everything, in the name of our Lord Jesus Christ.
> EPHESIANS 5:18–20

There is a genuine debate in commentaries as to whether Paul meant 'sing and make music *with* your heart', meaning with your whole heart, letting your worship be an expression of the love and devotion and gratitude that you feel towards Christ; or whether he meant 'sing and make music *in* your heart', describing the location of our worship, so it is not just going on with the outward movement of mouths singing, hands rising, knees bending, heads bowing, and so on, but it is really happening in our hearts, at the centre of our being and at the core of who we are. Remember how Jesus criticised the Pharisees and said: 'These people honour me with their lips, but their hearts are far from me' (Matthew 15:8)?

As both readings of that phrase are possible, and both are actually true, it would be wise to embrace both meanings. Christian worship is to be passionate and heartfelt, singing psalms and hymns and spiritual songs with hearts full of deep love and gratitude to the Lord who has saved us; *and* it is to be done from the core of our being, from the centre of our personality, with integrity, commitment, surrender and obedience.

The worship leader Matt Redman wrote a famous song while he was on the staff of St Andrews, Chorleywood, entitled 'The heart of worship'. In it, he acknowledges that worship is much more than just music and songs sung to God. He talks of the way the Lord looks within us and searches our hearts to see if we are worshipping with sincerity and heartfelt devotion.[73] This shouldn't cause us to be over-spiritual or desperately pious as we come to worship – God knows us through and through and he's not the slightest bit impressed by sudden bouts of piety! Genuine confession and heartfelt repentance are core ingredients in our times of worship too. But it is important to remember that, as we worship together, God is looking into our hearts and asking us: do you really love me? Is this coming from the core of your being? And will your life through the week match up with your lips?

This leads us to another very similar passage to the Ephesians passage quoted above, where Paul seems to be repeating himself, only this time to the Colossians. But there is an important difference that is worth noting:

Let the message of Christ dwell among you richly as you teach and admonish one another with all wisdom through psalms, hymns, and songs from the Spirit, singing to God with gratitude in your hearts. And whatever you do, whether in word or deed,

> do it all in the name of the Lord Jesus, giving thanks to God the
> Father through him.
> COLOSSIANS 3:16–17

To the Ephesians he emphasised 'Be filled with the Spirit' as the key to heartfelt worship on Sunday and through the week. Here in Colossians, it is 'Let the word of Christ dwell in you richly'. Again, we don't have to make a choice, but embrace both resources in helping us to be 'pure in heart'. God's word and God's Spirit are the secrets to living and worshipping with integrity. We desperately need both: to be filled with the Spirit enables us to be transformed into the likeness of Christ and empowered to live and worship with integrity; letting the word of Christ dwell in us richly teaches and trains us in godly living (2 Timothy 3:16–17; Psalm 119:9–11).

We have seen that the 'pure in heart' are those who display a consistency of behaviour and a singleness of purpose *in public and in private*. Both of these spheres matter hugely for the credibility of the gospel and the honour of God's name. It can safely be said that when public or private integrity has been lacking among God's people, the cause of Christ has struggled. But where people can see that Christ's followers have a consistency of character in personal holiness and public morality, in worship and at work, the kingdom advances and the truth of the gospel is self-evident. Robert Murray M'Cheyne, the 19th-century Scottish Presbyterian pastor, was right when he said: 'The greatest need of my people is my personal holiness.'[74] Jesus would agree, adding, I suspect, that the greatest need of *the world* is for my people to be 'pure in heart', living consistently in public and in private.

Personal reflection

Blessed are the pure in heart, for they will see God

- Am I pure of heart? Are my intentions pure? Do I say 'yes' and 'no' as Jesus did?
- There is a purity of heart, of lips, of eyes, of body: do I seek to cultivate all these kinds of purity that are so necessary?
- The clearest opposite of purity of heart is hypocrisy. Whom do I seek to please by my actions: God or other people?

Prayerful response

The 'Collect for Purity' is 'the name traditionally given to the collect prayed near the beginning of the Eucharist in most Anglican rites. It appears in Latin in the 11th-century Leofric missal and was part of the preparation prayers of priests before Mass. Thomas Cranmer translated the prayer into English and from there it has entered almost every Anglican prayer book in the world', first appearing 'in the *First Prayer Book* of Edward VI (1549), and carried over unchanged... [into] *The Book of Common Prayer* (1662)'.[75]

Almighty God, unto whom all hearts be open, all desires known, and from whom no secrets are hid: cleanse the thoughts of our hearts by the inspiration of thy Holy Spirit, that we may perfectly love thee, and worthily magnify thy holy name: through Christ our Lord. Amen

Discussion questions for small groups

Pure in heart

Starter (15 mins)
- In which situations do you find it necessary to wear a mask and put on a show, making yourself out to be someone different from who you are?
- Why is this peer-group pressure so important to you?

Main course (60 mins)
- What is Jesus commending in this beatitude?
- In which sections of the sermon on the mount is this underlined and illustrated?
- How important is personal integrity on your frontline, in your workplace or wherever God has placed you?
- Do you think we should expect a match-up of personal and public life from our political leaders?
- How can the church free itself from accusations of hypocrisy? Can you give examples?
- If God is 'looking into our hearts' when we worship, what does he hope to see?
- How can we match up our life with our lips?

Dessert (15 mins)
- Allow the Lord to search your heart to find the areas where you are tempted to wear a mask, to lack consistency of life and lips, and to have double standards.
- Ask for cleansing and forgiveness, and reach out to him to receive his healing touch.
- Pray to be filled with the Spirit so that your worship and your life may honour God with a glorious consistency, bringing honour to his name.

7

LIVING WITH RECONCILIATORY LOVE

Blessed are the peacemakers, for they will be called children of God.
MATTHEW 5:9

Divided world

Looking at the social landscape of Western civilisation, it is not hard to see how divided we are in so many ways. Social class is still the major category of social division, despite the inadequacies of applying Marxist definitions now to the new world of international markets and global economies. Other factors are also very significant in fostering division: race, nationality, gender, religion, political persuasion, age, location, education, employment, mobility, access to technology, health and disability all contribute to differences of outlook and value systems, sometimes leading to conflict. Social divisions have close links to social inequality, because these divisions often indicate the degree to which people can access resources and opportunities. The 'under-classes' of migrant, prison and homeless communities are below the radar of mainstream society much of the time, except when there is an outbreak of violence or social disruption. While national and cultural identities can and should be celebrated, for example in the competitive rivalries of sport, these also often spill over into national rivalries, ethnic struggles and social conflict. Tragically, the end of the Cold War has ushered in a new era of wars centring on the Middle East, the Baltic States and the Far East.

The rise of a radical Islamic fundamentalism has been the most concerning aspect of international politics in the last 50 years.The two main expressions of this have been Al Qaeda and ISIS, who have a common ideological opposition to the West, but have very different approaches to waging jihad and inflicting violence. Al Qaeda's primary focus of opposition has always been the United States, whereas ISIS has waged war on 'apostate Shi'ite regimes' such as Syria and Iraq in an attempt to create a 'pure', radical Islamic state. Using social media and online propaganda, ISIS has recruited thousands of young jihadists from all over the world. In a speech in June 2013, the ISIS leader, Al-Baghdadi, is reported to have said:

> Rise, oh lions of the Islamic State in Iraq and the Levant, and cure the frustration of the believers and attack the hateful Rafidah [Shi'ites], the criminal Nusayris, the Party of Satan [Hezbollah] and those who come from Qum, Najaf and Tehran. Show us from them blood and body parts and tear them apart, for we have known them when we have met them to be cowards. The Islamic State in Iraq and the Levant remains as long as we have a pulse or an eye that blinks.[76]

We certainly live in a fragmented and broken world. It all seems a long way from John Lennon's idealistic optimism expressed in his famous song 'Imagine'. Here, he invites us to dream of a world where all the barriers that divide human beings, including religion, are broken down so there is nothing to kill or die for and 'the world will be as one', with people living in peace.[77]

While not agreeing with all his ideas, Christians also have a vision for world peace, of reconciliation between warring factions and unity among the peoples of the world. It is there in the original covenantal promise to Abraham that through his seed 'all the nations will be blessed' (Genesis 12:2–3). It is there in the messianic prophecies of Isaiah about 'every warrior's boot used in battle... will be destined for burning' (Isaiah 9:5) and 'the wolf will live with the lamb' (Isaiah 11:6). It is there in the last chapter of the Bible, in the vision of the

New Jerusalem, where there is a tree of life by the river, and 'the leaves of the tree are for the healing of the nations' (Revelation 22:2). But how is this possible? Is this not similar to Lennon's idealistic dreaming?

The Prince of Peace

The peace of God is a much bigger concept in the Bible than 'feeling peaceful' or having 'peace of mind'. The Hebrew word is *shalom*, meaning wholeness, completeness and well-being, and in the Old Testament it is a key blessing from God through his covenant with Israel (Numbers 25:12). The blessing of *shalom* means a spiritual wholeness of a close relationship with God himself, as well as a social well-being whereby relationships with family and friends are restored and wholesome in the wider community. It results in an inner sense of well-being, knowing we are loved by God and those around us, and experiencing joy and purpose in our lives. If the fall of humanity, described in Genesis 3, caused a loss of relationship with God and neighbours, then *shalom* undoes the negative consequences and restores God's people to that place of spiritual wholeness and social well-being.

This is what God's people in the Old Testament longed for more than anything else, and they definitely experienced periods of *shalom* at various times: when they finally settled into the promised land (Joshua 21:43–45), when King Solomon had built the temple in Jerusalem and reigned over a period of peace and prosperity for Israel (2 Chronicles 5—9) and when the exiles in Babylon had finally returned to their land and rebuilt their city and temple in Jerusalem (Nehemiah 12:40–43). Yet it never seemed to last, and before long they were back into their old cycles of disobedience, disloyalty and idolatry. They broke the covenant, they worshipped other gods and they disobeyed God's laws and commandments, and so there were constant wars with the neighbouring nations and internal conflict and disharmony. They forfeited the blessing of *shalom*.

So it became a key element in the writings of the prophets that the hope of a coming messiah would usher in a new period of *shalom*, deeper and more permanent than ever before. Isaiah 9 is a classic example: the people who walked in darkness have seen a great light (v. 2); there is great rejoicing (v. 3); there is an end to warfare and subjection to foreign rulers (vv. 4–5) because the Messiah is born who is called 'the Prince of Peace' (v. 6); and there will be no end to his rule of peace (v. 7). This is a *shalom* that will last for ever.

It should not surprise us, therefore, that when the Messiah does come, the angels announce to the shepherds in the birth narratives: 'Glory to God in the highest heaven, and *on earth peace* to those on whom his favour rests' (Luke 2:14). Jesus' parting gift to the disciples as he prepares to go to the cross is the gift of *shalom* ('Peace I leave with you; my peace I give you', John 14:27). And in many of the resurrection appearances of Jesus, the first thing that he says to his bewildered and frightened disciples is 'Peace be with you' (Luke 24:36).

The apostle Paul portrays *shalom* as being one of the main blessings of the gospel because the death and resurrection of Christ have enabled us to come back into relationship with God (Romans 5:1; Colossians 1:20) and also enjoy restored relationships with those around us (Galatians 3:26–29). The writer of the Hebrews describes the Lord as 'the God of peace, who through the blood of the eternal covenant brought back from the dead our Lord Jesus, that great Shepherd of the sheep' (Hebrews 13:20). The early church experienced wonderful times of *shalom* (Acts 2:42–47; 4:32–35; 9:31) and Christians are told to have their 'feet fitted with the readiness that comes from the gospel of peace' (Ephesians 6:15). One of the consequences of bringing everything to God in prayer, says Paul, is that 'the peace of God, which transcends all understanding, will guard your hearts and your minds in Christ Jesus' (Philippians 4:7). Here is God's gift of *shalom* being given in a deeper and more permanent way under the new covenant.

Peacemaking, therefore, is first and foremost a divine activity, through which God makes peace with humankind through the gift of his Son, and also brings peace to the world by breaking down the dividing walls of hostility between communities (Ephesians 2:14–18). Graham Cole, professor of theology at Trinity Evangelical Divinity School, in *God the Peacemaker* (IVP, 2010), provides a deep reflection on Colossians 1:20, which says that God is reconciling all things in Christ. His thesis is that the greatest need in the world is *shalom*, and that God intends to make peace in the universe through a great plan of salvation focused on the cross of Christ. This means that peacemaking becomes one of the main priorities for the followers of Christ: we too try to help people to make their peace with God, and we try to bring peace and reconciliation between people, communities and nations who are divided. This brings us to the seventh beatitude.

Blessed are the peacemakers

In view of the above, it is clear that God himself is the great peacemaker, and that any concept of us being peacemakers must focus on what God has done in Christ to bring us peace. Also, seeing that one of the greatest blessings that will be enjoyed when the Messiah comes, according to Isaiah (chapters 9, 11 and 61), will be the wholeness and well-being of restored relationship with God, then to be peacemakers will involve calling people back into fellowship with their creator by announcing the gospel (Romans 10:14–15). This is the primary task of God's people and it would have been impossible for Jesus not to have included it in his call for his followers to be peacemakers. By this measure, Dr Billy Graham, the late international evangelist, was arguably the greatest peacemaker of recent Christian history. He preached to hundreds of thousands of people in the second half of the 20th century and my own mother came to a personal faith in Christ after hearing him at Wembley in 1973. Speaking about this beatitude, he said:

> Peace can be experienced only when we have received divine pardon – when we have been reconciled to God… 'There is no peace, saith my God, to the wicked' (Isaiah 57:21). But through the blood of the cross, Christ has made peace with God for us and is himself our peace.[78]

There is also the relational aspect of peacemaking towards other people that flows from this restored relationship with God: as Robert Guelich says, 'The peacemakers of [Matthew] 5:9 refer to those who, experiencing the *shalom* of God, become his agents establishing his peace in the world.'[79] Jesus would have been aware that the Zealots, the Jewish revolutionaries of his day, were wanting a violent overthrow of Roman rule in order to usher in the kingdom of God, and they believed that their willingness to take up arms to overcome oppression was a sign of their being 'true sons of God'. Not so, says Jesus: it is the peacemakers who are the true sons of God. This will be re-emphasised later in the sermon with teaching about turning the other cheek and loving your enemies (Matthew 5:38–48).

So, our call to peacemaking in the conflict areas of the world flows from the peacemaking of God through Christ. There is a divine logic here because, in the saving work of Christ, God is 'putting the world to rights', undoing the effects of the fall and healing the wounds of our hurting and broken world. This is the metanarrative, the big story of a God who 'so loved the world, that he gave his one and only Son' (John 3:16). Put simply, God is reclaiming his world, and his followers are to join with him in that process.

This is not to say that others who are not Christians have no part in this process – in fact, when you look down the roll of the 'world's greatest peacemakers', many of them are people of other faiths or no faith. Their contributions have been hugely significant: Mikhail Gorbachev, whose reforms in the Soviet Union led to the end of the Cold War, and was therefore awarded the Nobel Peace Prize in 1990; Mahatma Gandhi, who led the non-violent movement of Indian independence; Lech Walesa, the leader of the Polish Solidarity

Movement, who was the main catalyst in ending communist rule in Poland and was awarded the Nobel Peace Prize in 1983; Diana, Princess of Wales, who worked with many charities to get landmines banned, support those affected by the AIDS epidemic, and raise awareness of those suffering with bulimia and suicidal tendencies by speaking openly about her own experiences; Malala Yousafzai, the schoolgirl in Pakistan who survived an attack by the Taliban to champion universal access to education and who was nominated for the Nobel Peace Prize in 2013, the youngest person ever to be considered, for example. These show that there is a wider human longing for peace and reconciliation and, as creatures made in the image of God, anyone is able to reflect the nature of God, the great peacemaker. In that sense, peacemaking might be considered to be a 'creation' mandate, part of our human responsibility to be responsible stewards over the whole of creation.

And yet we have also seen that the biblical concept of *shalom* is also a 'salvation' mandate, given to the Israelites under the old covenant and given to Christians under the new covenant. And therefore it is heartening to see the names of many followers of Christ among those listed as the world's greatest peacemakers: Leo Tolstoy, the novelist who interpreted the ethical principles of Jesus in the sermon on the mount very literally, creating a non-violent philosophy of peacemaking, which later influenced Gandhi and Martin Luther King; Desmond Tutu, the Archbishop of Cape Town who campaigned against apartheid as well as for other humanitarian causes; Mother Teresa, the founder of the Missionaries of Charity in Calcutta, for her work with the destitute and dying, who put herself in the middle of gunfire to save 37 children in Beirut in 1982 and who was awarded the Nobel Peace Prize in 1979; Pope John Paul II, who became Poland's first pope and touched the world by his gentle kindness; Maria Ida Giguient, who has worked for the Catholic Relief Services (CRS) and has devoted over two decades to bringing peace to Mindanao and East Timor, continuing her peace-building efforts by training various international groups in overcoming violence.

The ministry of reconciliation

Two personal moments brought me close to two of the finest peacemakers in living memory, who both owed an allegiance to the Prince of Peace, from whom their inspiration and motivation flowed. The first moment was when my family was on holiday in the USA and we stood on the steps of the Lincoln Memorial, in the precise spot where Martin Luther King made his famous 'I have a dream' speech to 250,000 civil rights supporters on 28 August 1963.

Martin Luther King Jr was born in 1929, at his family home in Atlanta, Georgia. His grandfather was a Baptist preacher and his father was pastor of Atlanta's Ebenezer Baptist Church, and King himself became pastor of a Baptist church in Montgomery, Alabama, having obtained a Bachelor of Divinity degree from Crozer Theological Seminary in 1951, and then his Doctor of Philosophy from Boston University in 1955. It was while at seminary that he became acquainted with Gandhi's philosophy of non-violent social protest, and, following a trip to India in 1959, he became convinced that non-violent resistance was the most potent weapon available to oppressed people in their struggle for freedom.

Following a black bus boycott, King gained a national reputation as the leader of the civil rights movement in America and became a national hero. His goal was to bring to an end the system of segregation in every aspect of public life – in the workplace, in shops, on public transport, at public toilets and drinking fountains, and such like. He was awarded the 1964 Nobel Peace Prize for his efforts before his untimely death, by assassination, in 1968 at the age of 39.

This is a small section of the speech that he made on that day, and standing there myself brought home the challenge of being a peacemaker wherever God calls me. It is worth noting how his words are infused with Christian vocabulary and biblical concepts, showing where his roots lay. The biblical quotation is from Isaiah

40:4–5, which we have seen is one of the key Bible texts that form the backdrop for the beatitudes:

> I have a dream that one day, down in Alabama, with its vicious racists, with its governor having his lips dripping with the words of 'interposition' and 'nullification' – one day right there in Alabama little black boys and black girls will be able to join hands with little white boys and white girls as sisters and brothers. I have a dream today!

> I have a dream that one day every valley shall be exalted, every hill and mountain shall be made low. The rough places will be made plain, and the crooked places will be made straight. And the glory of the Lord shall be revealed and all flesh shall see it together. This is our hope. This is the faith that I go back to the South with.

> With this faith, we will be able to hew out of the mountain of despair a stone of hope. With this faith, we will be able to transform the jangling discords of our nation into a beautiful symphony of brotherhood. With this faith, we will be able to work together, to pray together, to struggle together, to go to jail together, to stand up for freedom together, knowing that we will be free one day…

> When we allow freedom to ring – when we let it ring from every city and every hamlet, from every state and every city, we will be able to speed up that day when all of God's children, black men and white men, Jews and Gentiles, Protestants and Catholics, will be able to join hands and sing in the words of the old Negro spiritual: 'Free at last! Free at last! Thank God Almighty, we are free at last!'[80]

The other personal moment was a family trip to Cape Town in 2016, when we visited Robben Island and I stood in the doorway of the tiny cell where Nelson Mandela was imprisoned for the first 18 years of his 27 years in jail. The prison had formerly been a leper colony off the coast of Cape Town, and his cell was without a bed or plumbing. He was forced to do hard labour in a lime quarry and, as a black political prisoner, he received scantier rations and fewer privileges than other inmates.

He was raised and schooled as a Methodist, an experience he fondly remembered. In school, Mandela studied law and became one of South Africa's first black lawyers. In the 1950s, he was elected leader of the youth wing of the African National Congress (ANC), and was involved in peaceful protests. However, when these protests were met with intimidation and violence from the government, Mandela organised a secret military movement, which led to a government ban on the ANC and to his subsequent imprisonment.

Although he was sentenced to life in prison, he was released early when the ANC became legal again. Subsequently, he became the first black and democratically elected president of South Africa from 1994–99. He did everything in his power to heal the wounds of the apartheid years and work with the former white minority. Mandela became a global symbol of reconciliation and peace and was awarded the Nobel Peace Prize in 1993 (jointly with former president F.W. de Klerk) for peacefully dismantling the apartheid regime and laying the foundation for democracy.

Mandela was a committed Christian who chose to be quiet and retiring about his faith in public, for fear of using religion as a political tool as the apartheid regime had done. In his autobiography, *Long Walk to Freedom* (Abacus, 1994), he talked of his early experiences with Christianity, praising the way it engaged with the society: 'The church was as concerned with this world as the next: I saw that virtually all of the achievements of Africans seemed to have come about through the missionary work of the church.'[81] At a religious conference in 1999, he said: 'Without the church, without religious institutions, I would never have been here today... Religion was one of the motivating factors in everything we did.' The president of the South African Council of Churches, Bishop Johannes Seoka, said of him: 'He was a man of great faith – he believed in God – but he was bigger than one denomination, even though he was a Methodist.'[82]

Upon his release from prison, Mandela took opportunities to speak at several Christian gatherings. At one of these, the Zionist Christian Church's Easter Conferences in 1994, he spelled out the links between Christ and the work of reconciliation and peacemaking, beginning his speech with a reading of the beatitudes:

> Easter is a joyful festival! It is a celebration because it is indeed a festival of hope! Easter marks the renewal life! The triumph of the light of truth over the darkness of falsehood! Easter is a festival of human solidarity, because it celebrates the fulfilment of the Good News! The Good News borne by our risen Messiah who chose not one race, who chose not one country, who chose not one language, who chose not one tribe, who chose all of humankind!

> We pray with you for the blessings of human solidarity, because there are so many who wish to divide us! We pray with you for the blessings of reconciliation among all the people of South Africa!

> We pray with you so that the blessings of peace may descend upon South Africa like a torrent! We pray with you that the blessings of love may flow like a mighty stream![83]

Following the legacy of King and Mandela, there are many excellent and thought-provoking guides to the ministry of reconciliation and peacemaking. One example would be *Reconciling All Things: A Christian vision for justice, peace and healing* by Emmanuel Katongole and Chris Rice (IVP, November 2008), who were, at the time of writing, co-directors of the Centre for Reconciliation at Duke Divinity School, North Carolina. Believing that the church has not always fulfilled its calling to facilitate reconciliation in the world, they offer:

> ... a comprehensive vision for reconciliation that is biblical, transformative, holistic and global. They... bring solid, theological reflection to bear on the work of reconciling individuals, groups and societies. They recover distinctively Christian practices that will help the church be both a sign and an agent of God's reconciling love in the fragmented world of the 21st century.[84]

Another would be James O'Dea in his book *Cultivating Peace: Becoming a 21st-century peace ambassador* (Shift Books, May 2012), in which he explores in depth the mission of building a global culture of peace. Although not writing from a specifically Christian point of view, he goes beyond techniques of conflict resolution to provide a holistic approach to peace work, covering the cultural, spiritual and scientific dimensions, and is helpful 'even for those who have never considered themselves peacebuilders'.[85]

It goes without saying that, for us to be effective peacemakers in the world, we must be at peace among ourselves within the Christian community. We need to repent of entrenched divisions and our tendency to divide over secondary issues and remember how Jesus prayed his heart out for unity among his followers in his high priestly prayer recorded in John 17. It must be a principled unity around the truth of God's word (v. 17) and we must all be able to submit to the authority of scripture as our rule and guide for Christian life and belief. But this must not be an excuse for us to separate ourselves from other believers over trivial doctrinal differences, but instead practise the saying that appeared for the first time in Germany around 1627 among peaceful church leaders of the Lutheran and German Reformed churches, and then found a hearty welcome among moderate divines in England: 'In essentials unity; in non-essentials liberty; in all things charity.'[86]

Pete Grieg, pastor and founder of the 24-7 Prayer movement, wrote an impassioned plea to the UK church in November 2016, saying:

> We find ourselves, at a time of European fragmentation, on the eve of the Reformation's 500th anniversary, coming together in unity from many nations and denominations to pray for the re-evangelisation of the continent. Perhaps it's time for Europe to rediscover its identity by remembering where it came from. We are nations forged by the fires of the gospel: the crucible of Christianity for a millennium.

He then cites the MORI poll which showed the church to be, positively, the most socially and culturally diverse community in the UK. He adds:

> With multiculturalism failing and protectionism proliferating, it is fantastic news that the church can stand as a prophetic example of reconciliation between different cultural, political and socio-economic identities.[87]

Personal reflection

Blessed are the peacemakers, for they shall be called children of God

- Am I a peacemaker? Do I bring peace to different sides?
- How do I behave when there are conflicts of opinion or conflicts of interest?
- Do I strive always to report only good things, positive words, and strive to let evil things, gossip and whatever might sow dissension, fall on deaf ears?
- Is the peace of God in my heart? If not, why not?

Prayerful response

Use the famous prayer attributed to St Francis of Assisi, who was the founder of the Franciscan Monastic Order in the 13th century, and who went on preaching tours wearing a rough grey tunic with a cord round his waist, and greeted people with the simple words: 'God give you peace':

> Lord, make me an instrument of your peace.
> Where there is hatred, let me bring love.
> Where there is offence, let me bring pardon.
> Where there is discord, let me bring union.
> Where there is error, let me bring truth.
> Where there is doubt, let me bring faith.
> Where there is despair, let me bring hope.
> Where there is darkness, let me bring your light.
> Where there is sadness, let me bring joy.
> O Master, let me not seek as much
> to be consoled as to console,
> to be understood as to understand,
> to be loved as to love,
> for it is in giving that one receives,
> it is in self-forgetting that one finds,
> it is in pardoning that one is pardoned,
> it is in dying that one is raised to eternal life.[88]

Discussion questions for small groups

Peacemakers

Starter (15 mins)
- What areas of conflict in the world are you most concerned about? Say why you are concerned, explaining some of the issues behind the conflict.

Main course (60 mins)

- What does Jesus have in mind when he announces a blessing on the peacemakers, and why are they called 'children of God'?
- Can you explain how Christ's death makes peace between us and God and reconciles all things to himself (Colossians 1:19)? Have a try.
- Christ also breaks down the wall of hostility between people who have been divided (Ephesians 2:14–15). Have you experienced this? If so, share your examples.
- Why is there so much division in the church worldwide if we are all united in Christ, and how can we be proactive in 'maintaining the unity of the Spirit' (Ephesians 4:3–4)?
- Do you have unresolved conflicts and divisions in your own life, family or workplace? How could you be a peacemaker in these areas?
- What practical steps could you as a group take to bring peace to a troubled area of the world, perhaps in one of the areas mentioned at the discussion starter?

Dessert (15 mins)

- Praise and thank the Lord for the peace he has brought into your life through the saving work of Christ.
- Using phrases from Jesus' prayer for the church in John 17, pray for a deeper sense of unity and cooperation between Christians in your locality and across the world, and for the healing of ancient divisions.
- Ask the Lord to use you to bring peace and reconciliation to a troubled area of conflict that you know about.

8

LIVING WITH UNDAUNTED COURAGE

Blessed are those who are persecuted because of righteousness, for theirs is the kingdom of heaven.
MATTHEW 5:10

Counting the cost

Let me begin by asking some rather personal questions: what does it cost you to be a Christian? Where do you feel the pinch? In whose company do you feel awkward because of your allegiance to Christ? When do you feel your integrity is being challenged by something you are asked to do? When were you last ridiculed for speaking up about your faith or because you made a stand for something that mattered to you? Have you ever been overlooked, ostracised or ridiculed for being a committed Christian? If you were arrested for being a Christian, would there be enough evidence to convict you?

Those questions are not meant to make us feel guilty but to help us face up to the cost of being a Christian today. Jesus knew that being the Saviour of the world meant 'giving his life as a ransom for many' (Mark 10:45) and the prophet Isaiah had predicted that suffering and persecution were awaiting the Messiah: 'He was despised and rejected by mankind, a man of suffering, and familiar with pain' (Isaiah 53:3). Jesus never said it would be easy for his followers, explaining that we must be willing to share in his suffering if we want to be his disciples (Matthew 16:24; Mark 13:9–13). The New

Testament epistles reinforce this call to bear the cost of following Christ (Romans 8:18; 2 Timothy 2:3; Hebrews 12:2–3), to see it as a mark of authentic discipleship (Romans 8:17; Philippians 3:10; 1 Peter 4:13) and to even count it as 'pure joy' when we suffer various trials for his sake (James 1:2; Colossians 1:24).

Sharing in his sufferings: the early church

The early church quickly found that they should expect to encounter opposition and rejection in being associated with Christ. It begins in Acts 4, when the Jewish authorities in Jerusalem resent the presence of this new Christian/Jewish sect, so they arrest Peter and John, throw them into prison and warn them not to speak any more about Jesus. Their reply is unequivocally defiant: 'Which is right in God's eyes: to listen to you, or to him? You be the judges! As for us, we cannot help speaking about what we have seen and heard' (vv. 19–20). The same thing happens in Acts 5, only this time it is all the apostles being arrested and tried, and this time they get a severe beating along with the charge not to speak any more about Jesus. Their reaction is extraordinary: 'The apostles left the Sanhedrin, rejoicing because they had been counted worthy of suffering disgrace for the Name' (v. 41).

Sooner or later, there was going to be a head-on collision, and somebody was going to get killed; it happened to be sooner rather than later. In Acts 6, Stephen is arrested for preaching openly in Jerusalem, and in Acts 7 he gives his defence before the Jewish Sanhedrin. His speech provokes the court to drag him outside the city and stone him to death and he dies with the (rather dubious) privilege of being the first martyr of the Christian church, the first of many who laid down their lives for the sake of him who laid down his life for them. Following Stephen's death, a great persecution arose against the church in Jerusalem (Acts 8:1), headed up by Saul of Tarsus, who would later become a Christian himself and bear many wounds for his faith (2 Corinthians 6:3–10). Yet, in God's providence, this very persecution allowed the gospel to spread beyond Jerusalem because those who were scattered took the good news with them 'wherever they went' (Acts 8:4).

As the gospel spread further afield, particularly through Paul's missionary journeys, the church came into conflict with Rome. For the first 30 years after Christ's death, the Roman occupying authorities tolerated and protected the church as a Jewish sect, as they saw it to be. But as Christians began to make converts from among the Gentiles, and as the difference between Christianity and Judaism became clearer, the church forfeited its protection under Roman law. Christians became unwelcome and unwanted members of the Roman Empire, particularly when they refused to pay homage to the emperor as divine. Things came to a head under the mad Emperor Nero in AD64: wishing to find a scapegoat for the fire of Rome, he blamed the Christians. The Roman historian Tacitus describes what happened:

> An arrest was first made of all who pleaded guilty; then, upon their information, an immense multitude was convicted, not so much of the crime of firing the city, as of hatred against mankind. Mockery of every sort was added to their deaths. Covered with the skins of beasts, they were torn by dogs and perished, or were nailed to crosses, or were doomed to the flames and burnt, to serve as a nightly illumination, when daylight had expired.[89]

Apparently, Nero opened up his grounds to allow people to come and watch this spectacle of Christians being burned as human torches to illuminate his gardens. There followed, periodically, 250 years of violent persecution by the Roman authorities: for example, the Emperor Decius issued edicts that commanded all citizens of the Empire to sacrifice to the traditional Roman gods, and those who refused to obey would be executed. Consequently, an unknown number of Christians were imprisoned and killed, among them the bishops of Rome, Antioch and Jerusalem. Most visitors to Rome will have the Colosseum on their itinerary, and here Christians were thrown to lions and bears before 45,000 cheering spectators.

The story of the martyrdom of Polycarp, the elderly bishop of Smyrna in the second century, is deeply moving. He was a very caring and much-loved pastor to his flock, but in AD156 there was a local outbreak of persecution and twelve Christians were condemned to die in the arena. The crowd then began to clamour for the bishop: 'Polycarp to the lions!' they shouted. He was found and brought before the Roman proconsul, who urged him to deny his faith: 'Take the oath and I will let you go; revile Christ!' The bishop calmly and unswervingly replied: 'Eighty-six years I have served him, and he has done me no wrong – how can I blaspheme my king who saved me?'[90] The crowd were incensed by his confession of Christ so, rather than wait for the wild beasts, they demanded that he should be burned alive. Hurriedly, logs were gathered together and a funeral pyre assembled. As the flames flashed up around him, Polycarp looked up to heaven, as Stephen had done, and praised and thanked God that he was counted worthy to take the cup of Christ's sufferings.

An anonymous letter to Diognetus was found, dating back to the second century, in which the writer describes the great paradoxes of Christian persecution:

> They love all men and are persecuted by all. They are unknown and condemned. They are put to death and restored to life… They are dishonoured, and yet in their very dishonour they are glorified; they are spoken ill of and yet are justified; they are reviled but bless; they are insulted and repay the insult with honour; they do good, yet are punished as evildoers; when punished, they rejoice as if raised from the dead.[91]

There is a very telling conclusion on this long period of suffering by the early church in Tim Dowley's *Handbook to the History of Christianity*:

> Despite periods of persecution, the church continued to grow. The storms of persecution made the flame of the gospel burn all the brighter... and helped purge the church of some of its more lukewarm members.[92]

Therefore Tertullian, one of the most famous second-century Church Fathers, was proved right: 'The blood of martyrs is the seed of the church',[93] because the willing sacrifice of their lives had led to the conversion of others and the growth of the church.

When the Roman Emperor Constantine converted to Christianity in AD313, he announced that 'it was proper that the Christians and all others should have liberty to follow that mode of religion which to each of them appeared best'.[94] This was a pivotal moment for the early church, whereby the Roman emperor now became the chief advocate and promoter of the Christian faith. In effect, Christianity became the official religion of the Roman Empire, which from one perspective was an extraordinary achievement in such a short period of time, from such humble beginnings, and was a step towards Christianity becoming a world faith. Yet winning the state patronage of the emperor understandably brought a new set of challenges for the church, which are outside the scope of this chapter.

Sharing in his sufferings: the modern church

In case we think that this was the end of persecution for the church, it is sobering to remember that more Christians were put to death for their faith during the last century than in all the previous centuries put together. In China, for example, Mao Zedong succeeded in his struggle for power in the Revolution of 1949 and established the communist People's Republic of China. He believed that Christianity was linked to Western colonialism and American hatred of communism, so his government expelled all foreign missionaries, closed down church organisations, destroyed all the Bibles they could find and subjected active Christians to harassment and humiliation. Those who defied the law and continued to practise their faith were imprisoned and executed. However, during these dark times, the church not only survived but grew: the Pew Forum on Religion and Public Life estimates over 67 million Christians in China today.[95] However, despite a more open and friendly approach to the West, the communist regime has continued and so has the persecution of Christians, particularly of the illegal house churches of China. This was brought to light by Brother Yun, a leader in the house church movement; in his book *The Heavenly Man*, he describes the treatment he received in March 1998, when the central government in Beijing learnt that the house churches were planning to unite to form one big denomination:

> The officers rushed at me, held me down and viciously kicked and beat me. They stamped on my legs and chest with their heavy boots, and pulled my hair and pistol-whipped me. My bones crunched and snapped under their savage blows and kicks. Then they produced the dreaded electric baton and tortured me with electric shocks. I was thrashed so severely that all that I could do was curl up and think of Jesus, trying not to pay attention to their blows… It was a miracle that I wasn't killed.[96]

This kind of severe persecution of Christians continues today in many countries of the world. Of the 50 countries of the world that are singled out by Open Doors, a Christian agency that supports the persecuted church, 'extreme' persecution is being experienced in ten countries, namely North Korea, Somalia, Afghanistan, Pakistan, Sudan, Syria, Iran, Iraq, Yemen and Eritrea. Another eleven are in the 'very high' category, including India, Saudi Arabia and Nigeria, and a further 19 are in the 'high' category, including China and Turkey. Their analysis of the World Watch List 2017 shows that millions of Christians around the world currently live their lives with varying levels of discrimination, violence and fear of arrest, and that this is the fourth year in a row that there has been a rise in the persecution of Christians worldwide, with Asia, particularly, showing a rapid rise.

Wars in the Middle East continue to catch Christians in the crossfire, while in Syria and Iraq Islamic militants continue to target Christians. In fact, Islamic extremism fuels persecution of Christians in 35 of the top 50 countries, although Hindu nationalism in India and Buddhist nationalism in Sri Lanka are also very opposed to the church.[97]

It is important to say at this point that Christians are not the only religious group experiencing persecution today, and the church must stand with and support any religious group that is being targeted for practising their faith, in the name of religious freedom, provided of course their practices are morally acceptable and consistent with upholding human rights. For example, there is a history of persecution of Muslims in Myanmar by the Buddhist majority government, with the largest Muslim minority, the Rohingyas, being recognised by the United Nations as one of the most persecuted groups in the world. The security forces have hounded them off their land, burned down mosques and committed widespread rape and looting. The story has been documented by Azeem Ibrahim in his book *The Rohingyas: Inside Myanmar's hidden genocide* (Hurst and Company, 2016). As I write this, violence in North Rakhine in recent weeks has caused a major refugee crisis, with over 400,000 Rohingyas fleeing from Myanmar to Bangladesh, to find safety across the border. Christians cannot, and should not, walk by on the other side and ignore this humanitarian crisis, any more than we can or should ignore the cries of the persecuted church.

Nor must we think that the church has an exemplary record when it comes to persecuting others. There is a long and sad history of Christians persecuting others, even fellow Christians with whom they had differences, and deep and heartfelt repentance is needed from all sections of the church. The Spanish Inquisition, for example, was established in the middle of the 15th century to maintain Catholic orthodoxy by identifying heretics, often under torture, and then it extended its activities to ordering Jews and Muslims to convert to Catholicism or leave Spain. Estimates reckon that 5,000 people were executed. Similarly, during the Reformation in Europe during the 16th century, Catholics and Protestants were guilty of putting each other to death for the sake of 'maintaining the true faith'. The Martyrs' memorial statue in Oxford commemorates the sad occasion when three senior Protestant Anglican clergy – the Archbishop of Canterbury, Thomas Cranmer, and two diocesan bishops, Latimer and Ridley – were burned alive at the stake by order of the Catholic Queen Mary. The relatively recent troubles in Northern Ireland were as much religious as they were political, with the two main communities self-identified as Catholic and Protestant, and it was often said that the people group most hardened to the gospel were British soldiers who had served a term of duty in Northern Ireland. Why would they want to give Christian faith a second thought after the violence, bombings and murders they had witnessed from two 'Christian' communities? They had a strong point!

How can we pray for our persecuted brothers and sisters around the world? Campus Crusade for Christ (also known as Cru) came up with five suggestions based on the book of Ephesians, because it was a letter written to persecuted believers, to show us how to pray for our brothers and sisters under attack:

- Pray that they would know the hope God gives (Ephesians 1:18)
- Pray that the Holy Spirit would strengthen them (Ephesians 3:16)
- Pray that they would know how much God loves them (Ephesians 3:17)
- Pray that they would know how to share the gospel (Ephesians 6:19)
- Pray that they would fearlessly tell others about Jesus (Ephesians 6:20)[98]

Finding courage

In the West, we don't experience physical intimidation, imprisonment or death for our faith in Christ, but it is certainly harder to be a Christian in our globalised, secular, pluralist and often dehumanising culture. The emphasis on globalisation leaves us feeling like pawns in the big game of markets and enterprise, with most of us at the mercy of the winds of change in the global economy. The secularisation of culture makes us feel like outsiders, aliens with a strange set of beliefs and values from another world, holding on to our convictions in private, but 'please don't bring them into the public square, or the office, or the staff room'. Pluralism makes it hard for us to hold on to the uniqueness of the revelation of God in scripture and the saving work of Christ in a world where all religious perspectives need to be treated equally in the marketplace of ideas and beliefs. 'That is your truth, and I have mine.'

All this can leave us feeling like strangers in a foreign land, similar to the exiles in Babylon, trying to navigate Christian discipleship in uncharted, post-Christian waters. The younger generation of Christians won't find it so strange because it is the only world they have known and the only cultural air they have breathed, and older ones (like me) will need them to help us to understand how to interpret this new world and navigate the future. But I suspect it will need to be a partnership of mutual support, because we can share with them our insights from the Bible, our understanding of the Christian tradition and our experiences of following Christ in a changing world. I am sure it was a partnership in Babylon too, with younger and older Jewish exiles helping each other to live courageously and thrive in the new cultural environment where God had placed them. This was the place where the prophet Isaiah brought the word of the Lord in Isaiah 61 – entitled in the NIV 'The year of the Lord's favour', providing hope and reassurance for the future.

The history of the persecuted church, and the fact that many Christians are still in those fires of suffering today, should inspire us to live courageous Christian lives, willing to count the cost of being a follower of Christ. We will need enormous courage to embody the vision of discipleship that Jesus has given us in the beatitudes. This is something that the Bishop of Oxford, the Rt Revd Steven Croft, highlighted when setting out a renewed vision for the Oxford Diocese at a conference for church leaders in 2017, using the beatitudes as the key biblical text upon which the future should be based. His third address was all about being a courageous church:

> To be a Christlike church means to become a more courageous church: to be wholehearted, to dare greatly together for the sake of the kingdom of God. In the language of the beatitudes, the church is to be courageous in being hungry and thirsty for justice. We are to be courageous in pursuing peace and reconciliation. We are to be courageous, like our Lord, in bearing the cost of our discipleship and the consistent boldness of our witness.

He added:

> I do not believe that this is a moment for the Church of England to mess around. We need to discern carefully what is right and then really go for it, to invest properly, to have the courage of our convictions and look for God to make an immense difference in the places where we serve.[99]

It is important to pause and reflect how countercultural, even offensive, this lifestyle will be in every period of human history and in every cultural context around the world. John Stott summarises it with his usual clarity and insight:

> The values and standards of Jesus are in direct conflict with the commonly accepted values of the world. The world judges the rich to be blessed, not the poor, whether in the material or in the spiritual sphere; the happy-go-lucky and carefree, not those who take evil so seriously that they mourn over it; the strong and the brash, not the meek and the gentle; the full, not the hungry; those who mind their own business, not those who occupy their time... 'showing mercy' and 'making peace'; those

who attain their ends even if necessary by devious means, not the pure in heart who refuse to compromise their integrity; those who are secure and popular and live at ease, not those who have to suffer persecution.[100]

Personal reflection

Blessed are those who are persecuted because of righteousness, for theirs is the kingdom of heaven

- Am I ready to suffer in silence for the gospel?
- How do I react when facing a wrong or an injury I have received?
- Do I participate intimately in the suffering of brothers and sisters who truly suffer for their faith or for social justice and freedom?

Prayerful response

Use the hymn written by Love M. Willis (1824–1908), where the author doesn't ask God for an easy, pain-free life, but for courage and strength to live for God's glory, whatever the cost:

Father, hear the prayer we offer:
not for ease that prayer shall be,
but for strength that we may ever
live our lives courageously.

Not for ever in green pastures
do we ask our way to be;
but the steep and rugged pathway
may we tread rejoicingly.

Not for ever by still waters
would we idly rest and stay;

but would smite the living fountains
from the rocks along our way.

Be our strength in hours of weakness,
in our wanderings be our guide;
through endeavour, failure, danger,
Father, be thou at our side.[101]

Discussion questions for small groups

Persecuted because of righteousness

Starter (15 mins)
- Have you ever been on the receiving end of unkindness or injustice, and how did it feel?

Main course (60 mins)
- How did Jesus himself embody this beatitude? What light does Psalm 22 throw on the sufferings of Christ?
- Do stories from the persecuted church, whether ancient or modern, inspire you? Share what you learn from their courageous suffering.
- In what ways do you feel under pressure as a Christian, and how do you respond?
- Do you think it is harder to be a faithful Christian today than 50 years ago? What has changed during this time?
- Can you think of times when God gave you courage to make a stand for Christ in some public setting? What effect did it have?
- How could you be more involved in supporting persecuted Christians in another part of the world?

Dessert (15 mins)

- Praise God for the patient suffering of Christ, who was led like a lamb to the slaughter.
- Pray for the persecuted church in some area of the world known to you, using the five prayer points from Ephesians mentioned above.
- Pray for courage to stand up for Christ in the public domain, among your friends, family and colleagues, whatever the cost.

9

THE SALT OF THE EARTH

You are the salt of the earth. But if the salt loses its savour,
how can it be made salty again? It is no longer good for
anything, except to be thrown out and trampled by men.
MATTHEW 5:13

Influencing the culture

It is also important to notice the flow of Jesus' teaching from the
beatitudes into the next section: living like this (Matthew 5:1–10)
means that we become the salt of the earth and the light of the world
(Matthew 5:13–16). John Stott again: 'If the beatitudes describe
the essential *character* of the disciples of Jesus, the salt and light
metaphors indicate their *influence* for good in the world.'[102] Living
differently enables us to make a difference. So we don't have to give
up and allow the world to shape us into its mould. We don't need to
throw up our hands in despair and say, 'Well, that's just the way it
is!' We don't allow ourselves to be overwhelmed by the flood tide of
social evil, moral collapse and religious indifference. We are being
called by Jesus into a humble, prayerful, determined engagement for
change. So what do these metaphors mean?

My parents used to talk of certain people as being the 'salt of the
earth', and they meant by that someone who was a good person
through and through, always kind and caring of others. The *Oxford
English Dictionary* officially defines the meaning of the phrase as 'a
person or group of people of great kindness, reliability, or honesty'.[103]
This should certainly be true of Christians if they are doing their best

to live out the beatitudes. However, when Jesus uses the phrase in Matthew 5:13, it seems that he had something more specific in mind: describing not just what they were like, but what kind of influence they might have on those around them.

The reason for this interpretation is that the primary use of salt in the ancient world was as a preservative: it was rubbed into meat to stop it putrefying. This highlights the 'preventative' aspect of Christian witness, as we live out the beatitudes in our families, communities and places of work. We are to hold back the destructive, degenerative forces of selfishness, greed, pride, anger and hatred. We are to challenge injustice and every kind of social evil that dishonours God and robs humankind of its dignity. To be the 'salt of the earth' means that nothing is 'off limits' for the church of Jesus Christ: we are to get stuck into the areas of life where there is greatest need, and to be present in places where humanity is most struggling. John Stott helpfully comments:

> We should not ask, 'What is wrong with the world?' for that diagnosis has already been given. Rather we should ask, 'What has happened to salt and light?' God intends us to penetrate the world. Christian salt has no business to remain snugly in elegant little ecclesiastical salt cellars; our place is to be rubbed into the secular community, as salt is rubbed into meat, to stop it going bad. And when society does go bad, we Christians tend to throw up our hands in pious horror and reproach the non-Christian world; but should we not rather reproach ourselves? One can hardly blame unsalted meat for going bad. It cannot do anything else. The question to ask is: 'Where is the salt?'[104]

A moving example of the early church being the salt of the earth happened in AD251 when a devastating epidemic swept through the Roman Empire, known as the Plague of Cyprian, killing roughly 5,000 people a day, and two thirds of Alexandria's population are said to have died. Rome was totally unprepared, practically, emotionally and spiritually, to help the sick or to deal with death on such a large scale. Their only strategy was to avoid all contact with those who had the disease, so the pagan priests, doctors and nobles fled the infected areas as quickly as they could.

In complete contrast, the Christians saw this tragedy as an opportunity to give testimony to the hope that was within them. They cared for the sick, washing them and supplying them with food on a daily basis, and their practical care actually helped to save lives because the simple provision of food and water helped some to survive when they would otherwise have been too weak to care for themselves. They consoled the dying, and buried those who died without funds for a proper burial. Understandably, this had a big impact on the pagan world, which was amazed by their selfless service and their willingness to risk their lives to save others. Charles Moore, a writer and member of the Bruderhof, an intentional community movement based on Jesus' sermon on the mount, reflected on this in an article entitled 'Pandemic love':

> The 'followers of the way', instead of fleeing the disease and death, went about ministering to the sick and helping the poor, the widowed, the crippled, the blind, the orphaned and the aged. The people of the Roman Empire were forced to admire their works and dedication.[105]

Losing our saltiness

There is a need, however, says Jesus, for salt not to lose it saltiness (Matthew 5:13). Apparently, chemists tell us, sodium chloride is a very stable compound, but it might lose its distinctive flavour if it becomes contaminated through being mixed with other impurities like, for example, road dust. It then becomes impure and even dangerous, neither tasting nor acting like salt, and so loses its effectiveness as a preservative. This is a constant danger for the followers of Christ. If we want to make a difference, influence society and see our friends, colleagues and families won for Christ, we have to avoid living compromised lifestyles, treating people unkindly, disrespecting the environment, ignoring the cries of the poor or harbouring deep resentments or prejudices. Instead, we have to retain a Christlike distinctiveness, and only then will people see our good works and give glory to our Father who is in heaven.

Perhaps the clearest and most poignant example of 'contaminated saltiness' was the church in Germany during World War II. There was a frightening level of compliance from both Catholic and Protestant denominations with National Socialism. The Nazis unified the Protestant churches into a single Reich church under the episcopal leadership of Ludwig Müller, a Lutheran with strong anti-Semitic opinions, who reorganised the church along Nazi lines: Hitler's *Mein Kampf* replaced the Bible in churches, members of the Nazi party only were allowed to preach and an 'Aryan paragraph' was adopted as one of its constitutional rules, which prohibited anyone of non-Aryan descent, including baptised Jews, from holding an official church post. These changes reflected the views of a movement within the Protestant churches known as 'German Christians' (*Deutsche Christen*), who embraced the slogan 'the swastika on our breasts and the cross in our hearts', worshipped Christ as an Aryan superman who had defeated the Jews, and idolised Hitler as a Germanic messiah. It was 'essentially Nazism in a Christian disguise… This travesty of Christianity was not imposed upon the church by the Nazis – indeed Hitler himself thought it rather silly'.[106] Worse still, the Protestant leaders issued an official pronouncement in December 1941 declaring that the Jews were beyond salvation by baptism owing to their racial constitution, were responsible for the war and were born enemies of the world and Germany.[107] The salt had lost its saltiness.

The same is true, sadly, of much of the German Catholic Church's compliance with and support of Nazism. The official position of the Vatican was one of detached disapproval, with Pope Pius XI negotiating a 'concordat' with Hitler in 1933, whereby the two would leave each other alone. The Pope did insist that an encyclical in 1937 was read in all churches in Germany, attacking Nazi ideology. However, there were many examples of German Catholic priests and bishops urging their flocks to embrace the values of the Third Reich, including anti-Semitism. Priests gave the Nazi salute at a Catholic youth rally in the Berlin-Neukölln stadium in 1933. Many Catholic publications exhorted their parishioners to comply with the Nazi authorities and join the armies of the Reich, and orders were given in all dioceses that nothing must interrupt or threaten the war effort. A pastoral letter by Bishop Kaller of Ermland in January 1941 reads:

> In this staunchly Christian spirit we also now participate wholeheartedly in the great struggle of our people for the protection of their life and importance in the world. With admiration, we look upon our army... as believing Christians, inspired by God's love, we faithfully stand behind our Führer who, with firm hands, guides the fortunes of our people.[108]

In addition to this was the compliance of senior Catholic prelates with the extermination of Jews, often by the way they spoke of them as enemies of God, killers of Christ and deservers of the fate that had befallen them. For example, Cardinal August Hlond, Primate of Poland, said in a pastoral letter in 1936, which was part of the official Catholic endorsement of the Nazi boycott of Jewish business in Poland and was read from pulpits across the country: 'It is a fact that the Jews are fighting against the Catholic Church, persisting in free thinking and are the vanguard of godlessness, Bolshevism and subversions.'[109]

In the world, but not of it

Could there be clearer examples of how the salt had lost its saltiness and how the church had been shaped and moulded by its cultural context, 'conformed to the pattern of this world' in Paul's words

(Romans 12:2)? There were, however, outstanding examples in Germany during the war where this was not the case. We have already noted Pope Pius XI's theological objections to Nazism. He saw racism as a form of idolatry and expressed his solidarity with persecuted Jews in Germany in a famous speech in 1938, when he said: 'Spiritually, we are all Semites.'[110] The most vocal opposition to Nazism from German Christians came from the 'Confessing Church' (*Bekennende Kirche* or BK), led by a Lutheran pastor called Martin Niemöller, who had originally been supportive of Hitler's rise to power but became disillusioned when he saw the direction the Third Reich was taking. Jonathan Hill describes the thrust of BK's ministry:

> The BK was essentially a form of unarmed resistance movement, which opposed the infiltration of Nazi racist and nationalist doctrines into Christianity… At a rally in Dahlem in late 1934, which was attended by 20,000 people, Niemöller declared, 'It is a question of which master the German Protestants are going to serve, Christ or another.'[111]

Many of the BK were persecuted or imprisoned, and Niemöller himself was arrested in 1937 and sent to the concentration camps.

Two other individuals stand out for their opposition to Nazism: one was Professor Karl Barth from Bonn University, who drafted the theological objections to the Reich in the Barmen Declaration of 1934, which formed the doctrinal underpinning of the BK. Here was a rejection of the state's authority over the church and a denunciation of Nazi anti-Semitism as a sin against the Holy Spirit. Needless to say, Barth lost his post at Bonn when he refused to swear an oath of allegiance to Hitler.

The other well-known German opponent of Hitler was Dietrich Bonhoeffer, a younger theologian who wrote in a letter to his closest friends on New Year's Day 1943:

We have been silent witnesses of evil deeds: we have been drenched by many storms; we have learnt the arts of equivocation and pretence; experience has made us suspicious of others and kept us from being truthful and open; intolerable conflicts have worn us down and even made us cynical. Are we still of any use? What we shall need is not geniuses, or cynics, or misanthropes, or clever tacticians, but plain, honest, straightforward men. Will our inward power of resistance be strong enough, and our honesty with ourselves remorseless enough, for us to find our way back to simplicity and straightforwardness?[112]

He is illustrating clearly the reality of salt losing its flavour, but also how the church can retain its saltiness: 'plain, honest, straightforward men', 'inward power of resistance', 'our honesty with ourselves', 'simplicity and straightforwardness'. It is not difficult to hear echoes of the beatitudes here (the poor in spirit, the meek, the pure in heart and the persecuted). He took his theological opposition to Hitler's regime to a deeper level by actively resisting the Reich's treatment of Jews and its military campaigns, even helping Jews to escape from Germany and launching an unsuccessful plot to assassinate Hitler, for which he was hanged in 1945. His martyrdom became a literal fulfilment of his unforgettable challenge to every Christian in his book *The Cost of Discipleship*: 'When Christ calls a man, he bids him come and die.'[113] In doing this, he showed us what it meant to be 'the salt of the earth'. An English officer who was imprisoned with him at Flossenbürg in Bavaria said he was 'one of the very few men that I have ever met to whom his God was real and close'.[114]

One of the most important places for us to be the salt of the earth is in the workplace, or wherever our front line of contact with the world is. Dorothy Sayers (1893–1957), the daughter of an Anglican priest and a British author famous for her detective novels, was passionate about the church seeing the workplace as a venue for glorifying God. In her article 'Why work?', she wrote:

In nothing has the church so lost her hold on reality as her failure to understand and respect the secular vocation. She has allowed work and religion to become separate departments... But how can anyone remain interested in a religion which seems to have no concern with nine-tenths of their life?... She has forgotten that the secular vocation is sacred... that every maker and worker is called to serve God in his profession or trade – not outside it.[115]

Among many excellent resources for churches to use to explore what it means to be salt and light in the workplace and on our front lines is a set of studies produced by Mark Greene at the London Institute for Contemporary Christianity entitled 'Fruitfulness on the frontline'. It explores how we can make a difference wherever we are by modelling godly character, making good work, ministering grace and love, moulding culture, being a mouthpiece for truth and justice and being a messenger of the gospel. It suggests: 'Daily life may never be quite the same.'[116]

Personal reflection

- Am I being the salt of the earth in the places God has placed me?
- Have I lost any of my saltiness?
- How can I keep my witness to Christ consistent, faithful and strong?

Prayerful response

This prayer, written by Revd Iona MacLean, was published by the development and relief agency of the Presbyterian Church in Canada:

Merciful God,
you call us to be salt of the earth and light of the world.
We confess that our witness is often bland and gloomy.

Forgive us when we fail to be an influence for good,
and when we condone or do what is wrong in your sight.
Help us to flavour the earth with righteousness
and to reflect the light of your love in a dark world;
through Jesus Christ, the Light of the world. Amen[117]

Discussion questions for small groups

The salt of the earth

Starter (15 mins)
- What are the similarities and differences between how salt was/is used in the first and 21st centuries?

Main course (60 mins)
- What was in Jesus' mind when he used the image of Christians being the salt of the earth?
- Can you think of any examples in the Old or New Testament when God's people had this kind on influence on those around them?
- When have Christians been 'salty' in the history of the church? Share some examples that you know about.
- Have you ever been in danger of losing your saltiness, and, if so, why?
- What spiritual disciplines might help us to keep salty?
- Where might you get involved more fully so that your saltiness might do its work? Is this something that you would do alone or with others?

Dessert (15 mins)
- Repent if you feel you have lost your saltiness in some way.
- Thank God for the privilege of being the salt of the earth, influencing the world for Christ.
- Pray that you can be effective and fruitful in the places where God has put you.

10

THE LIGHT OF THE WORLD

You are the light of the world. A town built on a hill cannot be hidden. Neither do people light a lamp and put it under a bowl. Instead they put it on its stand, and it gives light to everyone in the house. In the same way, let your light shine before others, that they may see your good deeds and glorify your Father in heaven.

MATTHEW 5:14–16

The guardians of the lamp

There was a fascinating and charming article in the *Daily Mail* in November 2014, called 'London's Last Lamplighters'. It invited us to imagine what London was like in the 18th-century world before the advent of gas-fired street lights.

> London was a dark city. In the 18th century, it was a brave walker who ventured out without servants to lead the way with a lamp in one hand and a cudgel in the other. Those who could not afford to keep servants would pay a few coins to... street urchins [to] walk ahead, carrying a stick with a rag dipped in tar and set alight... Those who couldn't afford to be guided in the dark took their chances – or rushed home before sunset.[118]

In other words, the streets of 18th-century London were not a safe place for residents or travellers, with the darkness of night providing a golden opportunity for villains, prostitutes and robbers. Violence and crime ruled the alleys and highways. But, with the advent of the gas lamp in 1807, London became a much safer place. One Victorian periodical, *The Westminster Review*, commented (rather cynically) that the introduction of the gas lamps had done more to eliminate immorality and criminality on the streets than any number of church sermons!

Today, London is ablaze with hundreds of thousands of electrically powered street lights and fluorescent lights left on all night in offices and shops, rightly causing environmental concerns about wastage and light pollution, but there are still 1,500 original gas lamps left in London, which continue to offer us a glimpse of the city from these times, when the gas lamps brought light and hope in a world of darkness and smog. Today, for example, the long avenue of Kensington Palace Gardens, lined now with embassies and billionaires' mansions, is entirely lit by Victorian gas lamps, so if you take a stroll down there after dark you will have an authentic experience of 19th-century London.

Who looks after these gas lamps? There once used to be hundreds of lamplighters who walked the streets at dusk, with long poles lit at the top to spark the gas lamps. But now there are just five of them – British Gas engineers – men in blue overalls at the top of ladders across the capital, from Richmond Bridge in the west, to Bromley-by-Bow in the east, servicing the mechanisms and polishing the glass lanterns. One of them insists that the title 'Lamplighter' does not do justice to the significance of their work. He says proudly: 'We are the guardians of the lamps.'

Five hundred years or so before the coming of Christ, the Israelites were called to be 'guardians of the lamp'. They lived in the deep darkness of exile, as we have seen: 'the people [the Israelites] walking in darkness… living in the land of deep darkness' (Isaiah 9:2). The spiritual darkness of this exile experience was utterly devastating and a living bereavement. Even the closeness and intimacy of God's presence seemed a dim and distant memory.

But Isaiah, as we know, is bringing a message of hope to the exiles caught up in this living nightmare: a great light is coming! They have seen a great light; and on them 'a light has dawned' (Isaiah 9:2). What is this great light? How shall we recognise it when it comes? The answer is an unexpected surprise: 'For to us a child is born, to us a son is given' (Isaiah 9:6). What's the good of that? How can a baby change anything? How can a child reverse the darkness and bring them once again into the light and warmth of God's presence? How can their world be sorted out? Because of who this child is, the prophet tells us: 'And he will be called Wonderful Counsellor, Mighty God, Everlasting Father, Prince of Peace.' These are titles that belong to God's special king, the Messiah, the one who comes as the Saviour that Israel had been waiting for:

> Of the greatness of his government and peace there will be no end. He will reign on David's throne and over his kingdom, establishing and upholding it with justice and righteousness from that time on and for ever.
> ISAIAH 9:7

So, a Saviour is coming, says the prophet, who will bring the light and warmth of God's presence to his people and, through them, to the world. His kingship will invade the darkness of sin, and guilt, and unbelief, and injustice and fear, and bring an end to alienation from God's presence. Receiving him will bring us into a new era of peace and joy, righteousness and justice. The Israelites must be the guardians of the lamp, and a light to the nations (Isaiah 49:6).

John picks up the light theme at the beginning of his gospel, reflecting the light imagery of Isaiah 9:

> The light shines in the darkness, and the darkness has not overcome it... The true light that gives light to everyone was coming into the world... He came to that which was his own, but his own did not receive him. Yet to all who did receive him,

to those who believed in his name, he gave the right to become children of God.

JOHN 1:5–12

And the godly old saint Simeon, waiting in the temple for the comforting of Israel (meaning the fulfilment of God's ancient promises), sets eyes on the child Jesus and is prompted into prophetic worship, highlighting the theme of light from Isaiah 49:6:

Sovereign Lord, as you have promised, you may now dismiss your servant in peace. For my eyes have seen your salvation, which you have prepared in the sight of all nations, a light for revelation to the Gentiles and the glory of your people Israel.

LUKE 2:29–32

Jesus himself will later declare: 'I am the light of the world. Whoever follows me will never walk in darkness, but will have the light of life' (John 8:12).

So a great light has dawned with the arrival of Jesus: this is the very light of God himself (Psalm 27:1), making himself known in the person of his Son, revealing his love and grace and forgiveness, and rebuilding broken lives and communities. The world is being put to rights. Jesus then entrusts his followers with the task of bearing witness to this light, being lamplighters in their homes, their communities and the wider world.

You are the light of the world. A town built on a hill cannot be hidden. Neither do people light a lamp and put it under a bowl. Instead they put it on its stand, and it gives light to everyone in the house. In the same way, let your light shine before others, that they may see your good deeds and glorify your Father in heaven.

MATTHEW 5:14–16

The phrase 'they shall see your good works and give glory to your Father who is in heaven' echoes Isaiah 61:3: 'They will be called oaks of righteousness, the planting of the Lord, for the display of his splendour.' This light must not be hidden, as if we were living through the Blitz and every curtain had to be tightly closed to avoid any light attracting the attention of enemy bombers. Instead, the light of Christ, shining in us, has to be on display, visible to a watching world, warmly inviting people into the light and joy of God's presence.

Within just ten years of the death and resurrection of Christ, these lamps had been lit all over the ancient world. This light had reached the three main centres of the Mediterranean: Alexandria, the greatest city in Africa; Antioch, the greatest city in Asia; and Rome, the capital city of the Empire. And from those three centres the light was set to spread throughout the ancient world so that, by the end of the third century AD, 'there was no area of the Roman Empire which had not been (to some extent) penetrated by the gospel'.[119]

Now the light of Christ shines in every nation of the world. Approximately one third of the global population owns an allegiance to Christ (estimated at 2 billion people) and, during the past century, the centre of gravity in the Christian world has shifted from the global north to the global south, so there are now far more Christians in South America, Africa and Asia (1.3 billion estimated) than in North America, Europe and Australia, Japan and New Zealand (860 million estimated).[120]

Will you be a lamplighter and guardian of the lamp, bringing the light and hope of Christ to those around you? In 1962, Adlai Stevenson, United States representative to the United Nations, paid tribute in the *New York Times* to former First Lady Eleanor Roosevelt, who had recently died, and said: 'Like so many others, I have lost more than a beloved friend. I have lost an inspiration. She would rather light a candle than curse the darkness, and her glow has warmed the world.'[121]

Peter Benenson, the English lawyer and founder of Amnesty International, had previously used this saying ('light a candle') at a Human Rights Day ceremony on 10 December 1961 and the candle circled by barbed wire has since then become the society's emblem. But it can be traced back to a publication in a 1907 collection titled *The Supreme Conquest and Other Sermons Preached in America* by William L. Watkinson. A sermon titled 'The invincible strategy' questioned the effectiveness of verbal attacks on immoral and ungodly behaviour and championed the importance of performing good works: 'But denunciatory rhetoric is so much easier and cheaper than good works, and proves a popular temptation. Yet is it far better to light the candle than to curse the darkness?'[122]

The original phrase has often been ascribed to Confucius or a Chinese proverb, but no compelling evidence has been found to support either of these. It would be safer to ascribe its origins to Jesus in Matthew 5:14, who acknowledged the deep darkness of his contemporary world, but invited his disciples to positively light a candle, choosing to live a countercultural lifestyle as outlined in the beatitudes and thereby bring blessing to the world and glory to God.

Salt and light in practice

Dr John Stott made a compelling case for 'lighting a candle' in his book *Issues Facing Christians Today*. This treatise went far beyond an intellectual exploration of the complex issues facing the global community at the end of the 20th century. In his opening chapters, he pleads with the church to get involved in making a difference in the world, on biblical and historical grounds. In his chapter on 'Alienation: Have we any influence?',[123] he uses Mathew 5:13–16 as his key biblical text for involvement and integration: Jesus' images of salt and light tell us that although Christians are called to be fundamentally different from the world (because we choose to live in the countercultural way of the beatitudes), we are, firstly, to permeate society and become immersed in its life, not standing aloof from all that is going on around us. Secondly, from this integration comes influence: 'Christians can hinder social decay and dispel the darkness of evil.'[124]

He then lists six ways we can 'be salt and light' in the places where God has placed us:

- Firstly, *by praying*, calling on God to move in power, interceding for our world, its leaders, and its challenges.
- Secondly, we can be salt and light *through our evangelism*, bringing the good news of the gospel to others, knowing that it is through Jesus Christ that the world is being remade and renewed.
- Thirdly, we can do this *through our witness to God's truth in the public square*, developing and contending for a Christian worldview and for a social, moral and biblical apologetic.
- Fourthly, we can be salt and light *by our protest*, identifying areas of social and moral evil and using public agitation as a weapon of exposure and change.
- Fifthly, *we can be examples* to those around us, showing them a lived-out embodiment of the better way, as Christ has shown us in the sermon on the mount, giving them a glimpse of life in the kingdom of God.
- Lastly, *we can join with others in small groups*, to work and pray for the advancement and growth of the kingdom of God in our local communities and our nation.

Here, Stott reminds us of an inspiring comment made by Robert Bellah, the American sociologist who specialised in the influence of religion and ethics on politics:

I think we should not underestimate the significance of a small group of people who have a new vision of a just and gentle world… the quality of a culture may be changed when two percent of its people have a new vision.[125]

James Davison Hunter, Distinguished Professor of Religion, Culture and Social Theory at the University of Virginia, wrote in his book *To Change the World* (2010) a penetrating and critical appraisal of Christian attempts to influence and change society in late modernity. Instead, he offered an alternative paradigm of Christian engagement with the world, developing a working theology of 'faithful presence' based on Jeremiah 29:4–7. Writing to the exiles in Babylon, Jeremiah explains that God had not abandoned Israel, but was still at work, fulfilling his purposes in and through this painful experience of exile. The prophet encourages them to settle down for the long term; to build, to plant, to marry, to have children and to seek the welfare of their city and their captors, praying that God would provide *shalom* in Babylon, blessing not only themselves as the people of God, but also the Babylonians themselves. Hunter says:

> The people of Israel were being called to enter the culture in which they were placed as God's people – reflecting in their daily practices their distinctive identity as those chosen by God. He was calling them to maintain their distinctiveness as a community but in ways that served the common good.

The images of 'salt' and 'light' in the New Testament also call us to this 'faithful presence' in the places where we live and work, however much we might feel like strangers in a foreign land. Hunter continues:

> A theology of faithful presence calls Christians to enact the *shalom* of God in the circumstances in which God has placed them and to actively seek it on behalf of others. This is a vision for the entire church – for the entire laity… in all vocations… and in all walks of life. In God's eyes, it is faithful presence that matters.[126]

In this way we become, not merely cultural critics, but cultural shapers, influencing society with the values of the kingdom of heaven, bringing glory to God and blessing to the world.

Personal reflection

- Where has God called me to shine a light for him?
- When do I tend to hide my light under a bushel, and why? How could I shine more effectively?
- Which of Stott's six suggestions might be right for me to take on board at this stage?

Prayerful response

St Columba (521–97) was an abbot and missionary in Ireland and Scotland. He set up a monastery on the island of Iona, and he and his fellow monks evangelised the Picts.

O Lord, give us we beseech you in the name of Jesus Christ, your Son, that love which can never cease, that will kindle our lamps but not extinguish them; that may burn in us and enlighten others.

O Christ, our dearest Saviour, kindle our lamps that they may evermore shine in your temple and receive unquenchable light from you that will enlighten our darkness and lessen the darkness of the world, in your name, Amen[127]

Discussion questions for small groups

The light of the world

Starter (15 mins)
- Start by trying to imagine a world without light – what would it be like, and what would we be unable to do?
- Now think of all the benefits that light brings into our lives... when are you most grateful for it?

Main course (60 mins)

- What does the Bible mean when it says that 'the Lord is my light' (Psalm 27:1), and what is significant about Jesus claiming to be 'the light of the world' (John 8:12)?
- In what ways did Jesus shine the light of God during his life and ministry?
- In our calling to be 'the light of the world', in what sense is it similar to the calling of Jesus, and how is it different?
- What is the secret of keeping our light shining brightly?
- Who do you know that is an inspiring example of a Christian in your workplace, community, learning environment or family, and how do they let their light shine in a way that makes a difference?
- Where could you light a candle rather than curse the darkness?

Dessert (15 mins)

- Take some time to gaze at the brightness and beauty of Christ. Use Revelation 1:12–18 to help you.
- Praise God for the opportunities you have to shine for Christ in the contexts where God has placed you.
- Pray to be 'guardians of the lamp', shining the light of Christ in areas of darkness, and lighting candles in situations of hopelessness and despair.

CONCLUSION: THE FACE BEHIND THE BEATITUDES

The beatitudes have taken us on a journey of healing, challenging us to address our chronic lifestyle dysfunction at a fundamental level: to receive from God his healing grace so that we can bring wholeness and healing to others. The journey starts with recognising our need of God (poor in spirit), expresses heartfelt sadness over the sin in our own lives and in our world (those who mourn) and results in a humble, gentle strength in our approach to others (the meek). We start to long for change and have a driving passion for the honour and glory of God (hunger and thirst after righteousness) and this involves bringing the healing grace of Christ to others (the merciful). This requires integrity, the matching up of how we behave in public and in private (pure in heart) and it allows us to bring *shalom*, God's peace, into situations of conflict and trouble (the peacemakers). All of this will be costly as we stand for God's righteousness in the world, requiring great courage to take up our cross, following in the steps of the Master. Here is the comprehensive portrait of a Christian disciple, as we noted earlier, and those who take this journey are richly 'blessed' both now and in the life to come. In living like this, we find our true selves: the people God made us to be and the reason why we were placed on this earth.

Will we live counterculturally in the way that Jesus calls us to? If so, then we will truly become the salt of the earth and the light of the world, making a difference in our communities, our workplaces and in our world. We become different in order to make a difference.

On the wall of a civic building in Washington, DC, there is a large plaque containing the Constitution of the United States, skilfully engraved in copperplate. When you first look at it, you see only the engraved words of the Constitution; then, on stepping back, so that the angle of the light changes, the face of George Washington appears, carved into the text. The reason is that he was not only the first president of the United States (1789–97) but he presided over the 1787 convention that drafted the US Constitution. In that sense, he is widely considered the 'father of the country', the driving force behind the formation and establishment of the US as a nation. His face is rightly and appropriately carved into the text.

I believe the same thing is going on with the beatitudes. They are a wonderful statement of the core values of Christian discipleship, a manifesto or constitution (if you like) for the church in every age, a call to a countercultural lifestyle, living differently to make a difference. They are simple yet sublime, revolutionary yet restorative, demanding everything from us and yet opening the treasures of the kingdom of heaven. They are worth building our lives upon as a foundation (remember that the sermon on the mount ends with the parable of the man who builds his house on the rock – he who hears my words and does them), and they are worth living and dying for. They are the essence of what it means to be fully human and fully alive. To lose our life, for Jesus' sake, is to find it (Matthew 10:39).

But let's stand back from the text as we close. Let's imagine the light changes and we notice something we didn't see at first. It is a face. It is the face of a carpenter's son from Nazareth. It is the face of someone who healed the sick, fed the hungry, loved those on the edges of society, challenged injustice, spoke truth to power and called people back into relationship with the God who made them. It is the face of someone who was despised and rejected by people, a man of sorrows and acquainted with grief. It is the face of a wounded healer, a divine physician, the doctor in the house who knows us through and through and is inviting us to live a countercultural lifestyle so that we can make a difference in the world and bring glory to our Father who is in heaven (Matthew 5:16).

How, then, is Jesus 'the face behind the beatitudes'?

Firstly, Jesus' face is here because he is the one who gives them to us; he sits down on the mountain, calls his disciples to himself and shares this way of life (Matthew 5:1–2). All the Bible commentators on this passage suggest deliberate allusions to Moses receiving the ten commandments on Mount Sinai and bringing the law of God to the people of Israel (Exodus 20). Here, now, on another mountain, is the second Moses, the greater prophet (Deuteronomy 18:15), bringing the rule of life to the people of God under the new covenant. We, too, must sit at the feet of the Master, placing ourselves under his authority and learning from him, for this is wisdom from heaven for life today in the 21st century. This is how we avoid being conformed to this world, but instead are transformed by the renewing of our minds (Romans 12:2). Jesus speaks the beatitudes for us today – but will we build our lives on this rock?

Secondly, Jesus' face is here because he embodies the beatitudes in his own life and ministry.

- He is poor in spirit, not in the sense of being sinful, but in the sense of knowing his need of God ('the Son can do nothing by himself, but he can only do what he sees the Father doing' – John 5:19).
- He mourns over the mess that the world is in, illustrated by his grieving over the death of Lazarus, his weeping over Jerusalem for its hardness of heart and his being sorely troubled in the garden of Gethsemane, as he faces the ordeal of the cross and drinking the cup of God's wrath to the last dregs for the sake of others.
- He is meek, being gentle and lowly in heart, and yet strongly determined to do God's will, setting his face steadfastly towards Jerusalem.
- He is hungry and thirsty for righteousness, seeking to expose the hypocrisy of the Pharisees and challenging the exploitation of the money changers in the temple courts.
- He is merciful and gracious towards the people who have got their lives in a mess – the beggar by the roadside, the lepers and the

prostitutes, the lost and the lonely – and he gives his life on the cross to rescue sinners.

- He is pure in heart, single-minded in his devotion to God and his ways, as his testing in the wilderness has proved.
- He is the peacemaker, making peace between us and God and between us and our fellow human beings, telling his disciples that *shalom* will be his parting gift (John 14:27; 16:33), and announcing 'peace be with you' at most of his resurrection appearances.
- He himself was persecuted, being hounded all the way to the cross by the religious leaders of his day and rejected by the very ones he came to save.

Therefore, Jesus is not asking of us anything that he himself has not done, for he has inhabited the beatitudes himself: he knows the cost of living like this, but he has shown it to be the way of life and peace. There is a total synergy between teacher and teaching in this call to discipleship.

Thirdly, Jesus' face is here because he enables us to live the beatitudes ourselves. We may well be thinking, having read this far, that this is an impossible ideal: who could live like this? We would fail every day at every point. Surely this is idealism taken to its limits, and therefore has a tinge of cruelty about it because it promises so much but is ultimately unrealistic and unachievable. Jesus has set the bar impossibly high and no one could ever reach these heights – and in one sense, of course, we would be right! None of us could do this on our own, relying on our own resources. But that is the point: we are not left on our own to muddle through, nor are we expected to 'pull up our socks' and live a miserable life trying to achieve the impossible, with a constant sense of failure and guilt. No: Jesus has sent his Spirit upon us to enable us to live lives that are worthy of the gospel, by which we have been saved. The same Holy Spirit who anointed the Messiah for his ministry (Isaiah 61:1; Luke 3:22) has now anointed the messianic community to live differently in the way that Jesus did (Acts 2:1–2). More than that, the Spirit has taken up residence in us and our bodies have become temples of the Holy Spirit (1 Corinthians 6:19). His power is made perfect in our weakness, and his grace is sufficient for us (2 Corinthians 12:9). He is able to do far more than all we can ask or think, by the power that is at work within us (Ephesians 3:20).

Canon David Watson was the gracious and gifted minister of St Michael the Belfry in York, under whose leadership the church grew into a centre for evangelism and renewal. He was also an international evangelist who conducted 58 missions in five continents between 1978 and 1983, and was responsible for leading hundreds of people to Christ. In his book *Discipleship*, he wrote about the importance of the beatitudes in his experience of being filled with the Spirit, which in turn equipped him to live this Christlike life:

> I was studying the beatitudes in Matthew 5. Over a period of two or three months, God took me, in my own experience, through the first four beatitudes. As his Spirit moved gently in my life, I began to see how spiritually poor I really was: I was bankrupt – in my heart I knew it, though I had often tried to cover it up with active Christian ministry. Then God caused me to mourn or weep for my spiritual poverty. I became genuinely concerned for my lack of love for Jesus, for my low level of faith, for my disobedience in various areas of my life. In this way, God made me meek, or humble before him. I saw myself at the foot of the cross, silently weeping for my spiritual poverty. Then I became very hungry and thirsty for spiritual righteousness. I longed for a life that would truly glorify God and please him in every way. Pride and complacency had been stripped away. It had been a painful and humbling experience, but God was preparing me to be filled with the Spirit.[128]

In his autobiography, he describes what happened next:

> I had a quiet and overwhelming sense of being embraced by the love of God. There were no startling manifestations... but it seemed that the presence of God filled the room in which I was

praying. I know that I had been filled with the Spirit, and I was bubbling over with new joy… God had met with me in a fresh way; of that I was certain.[129]

So, the beatitudes are not the 'impossible ideal' but the 'normal Christian life', made possible by the indwelling Spirit of God, who fills us with the love and power of God to do the will of the Father, flowing from the saving work of Christ. 'Be very careful, then, how you live… Understand what the Lord's will is… Be filled with the Spirit' (Ephesians 5:15–18). There is a ruthless logic there, which turns out to be the secret of Christian discipleship and witness, of living differently to make a difference.

NOTES

1 See www.drchatterjee.com.
2 www.mirror.co.uk/lifestyle/health/doctor-house-changes-lives-one-6843292
3 Quoted on www.doctoraseem.com/lifestyle-medicine-save-nhs-billions-halt-healthcare-crisis.
4 www.dailymail.co.uk/home/article-4672104/Yuval-Noah-Harari-s-dark-vision-future.html
5 J.D. Vance, *Hillbilly Elegy: A memoir of a family and culture in crisis* (HarperCollins, 2016).
6 www.episcopalnet.org/1928bcp/FBSMP.html
7 John Stott, *Christian Counter-Culture: The message of the sermon on the mount* (IVP, 1978), pp. 31, 54.
8 Craig A. Evans, *Matthew (New Cambridge Bible Commentary)* (Cambridge University Press, 2012), p. 103.
9 W.D. Davies and D.C. Allison, *Matthew (International Critical Commentary)* (T&T Clark, 1988), p. 438.
10 Robert Warren, *Living Well* (Fount/Harper Collins, 1998), p. xvi.
11 The whole sermon can be read here: www.cslewisinstitute.org/Becoming_More_Like_Christ_Stott.
12 R.T. France, *The Gospel of Matthew (New International Commentary)* (Eerdmans, 2007), p. 153.
13 E. Stanley Jones, *The Christ of the Indian Road* (Abingdon Press, 1925). Quotation found here: www.samsusa.org/2017/07.
14 See www.worldhappiness.report/ed/2018.
15 See www.lutheran-hymnal.com/lyrics/lw294.htm for the full hymn.
16 Davies and Allison, *Matthew*, p. 443.
17 See www.hymnsite.com/lyrics/umh361.sht for the full hymn.
18 *The Times*, Wed 12 July 2017.
19 This reflection and subsequent ones in the next seven chapters are from Raniero Cantalamessa's 'Examen of Conscience' based on the beatitudes. See do-not-be-anxious.blogspot.co.uk/2010/01/examination-of-conscience.html.

20 Peter Cozzens, *The Earth is Weeping* (Atlantic Books, 2017), p. 7.

21 Cozzens, *The Earth is Weeping*, p. 427.

22 Cozzens, *The Earth is Weeping*, p. 457.

23 Davies and Allison, *Matthew*, p. 448.

24 Evans, *Matthew*, p. 105.

25 Revd Jonathan Edwards and Sereno Edwards Dwight, *Memoirs of the Rev. David Brainerd: Missionary to the Indians on the borders of New York, New Jersey, and Pennsylvania* (S. Converse, 1882), p. 58.

26 Wesley Duewel, quoted on www.prayforrevival.org.uk/encourager20.html.

27 Charles Finney, quoted on www.prayforrevival.org.uk/encourager20.html.

28 Yeonmi Park, *In Order to Live: A North Korean girl's journey to freedom* (Fig Tree, 2015).

29 Read the full article at www.theguardian.com/media/2007/mar/04/broadcasting.bbc1.

30 Read the full article at www.relevantmagazine.com/culture/christians-have-mourn-injustice.

31 St Aldates, 'Rule of life', p. 11. You can view the booklet online at www.staldates.org.uk/resources/_Rule_of_Life.pdf.

32 www.bcponline.org/SpecialDays/ashwed.html

33 *The Guardian*, Letters, 6 July 2017, p. 32.

34 Stott, *Christian Counter-Culture*, p. 43.

35 Martyn Lloyd-Jones, *Studies in the Sermon on the Mount* (IVP, 1977), p. 65.

36 Stott, *Christian Counter-Culture*, p. 43.

37 France, *The Gospel of Matthew*, p. 66.

38 Max Hastings, *All Hell Let Loose: The world at war 1939–45* (Harper Press, 2011), p. 196.

39 Hastings, *All Hell Let Loose*, p. 268.

40 C. Plaxton, *Treasure of Salisbury* (The Abbey Press, 1971), p. 19.

41 Plaxton, *Treasure of Salisbury*, p. 15.

42 Plaxton, *Treasure of Salisbury*, p. 20.

43 Plaxton, *Treasure of Salisbury*, p. 16.

44 Plaxton, *Treasure of Salisbury*, p. 27.

45 Mother Teresa, *In the Heart of the World: Thoughts, stories and prayers* (New World Library, 1997).

46 The prayer can be found online here: www.catholicdoors.com/prayers/english5/p03408.htm.

47 www.vocabulary.com/dictionary/gluttony

48 '2016 world hunger and poverty facts and statistics': www.worldhunger.org/2015-world-hunger-and-poverty-facts-and-statistics.

49 www.christianitytoday.com/history/issues/issue-53/william-wilberforce-and-abolition-of-slave-trade.html?type=issuePrev&number=7&id=4196

50 www.christianitytoday.com/history/issues/issue-53/william-wilberforce-and-abolition-of-slave-trade.html?type=issuePrev&number=7&id=4196

51 en.wikiquote.org/wiki/William_Booth

52 www.salvationarmy.org.uk/history-william-booth

53 N.T. Wright, *Surprised by Hope* (SPCK, 2007), p. 205.

54 The prayer can be found at: www.worldprayers.org/archive/prayers/invocations/may_god_bless_you_with_a_restless.html.

55 James Swallow, *Nomad* (Zaffre, 2016), p. 166.

56 *Eye for an Eye*, 1995 (directed by John Schlesinger).

57 See www.hymnary.org/text/and_can_it_be_that_i_should_gain for the full hymn.

58 Bernard Ward, *St Edmund, Archbishop of Canterbury: His life as told by old English writers* (Sands, 1903), p. 52.

59 Ward, *St Edmund*, p. 53.

60 Ward, *St Edmund*, p. 137.

61 Corrie ten Boom, *Tramp for the Lord* (Berkley, 1978), pp. 53–55.

62 William Ury, *The Third Side* (Penguin Books, 1999), quoted on www.uccphilosoph.com/wiki/Gordon_Wilson.

63 See en.wikipedia.org/wiki/The_quality_of_mercy_(Shakespeare_quote) for the full speech.

64 See www.birminghamdiocese.org.uk/wp-content/uploads/2015/10/Year-of-Mercy-Pope-Francis-Prayer-2.pdf for the full prayer.

65 en.wikipedia.org/wiki/Integrity

66 See www.forbes.com/sites/amyanderson/2012/11/28/success-will-come-and-go-but-integrity-is-forever for the full article.

67 Davies and Allison, *Matthew*, p. 456.

68 Charlie Cleverly, *Epiphanies of the Ordinary: Encounters that change lives* (Hodder & Stoughton, 2013).

69 France, *The Gospel of Matthew*, p. 169.

70 Walter A. Elwell (ed.), *Evangelical Dictionary of Theology* (Marshall and Pickering, 1985), 'Heart', pp. 498–99.

71 See www.theguardian.com/books/2016/nov/15/post-truth-named-word-of-the-year-by-oxford-dictionaries for the full article.

72 www.theguardian.com/books/2016/nov/15/post-truth-named-word-of-the-year-by-oxford-dictionaries

73 Matt Redman, 'The heart of worship' (Thankyou Music, 1997).

74 www.mcheyne.info/quotes.php

75 See en.wikipedia.org/wiki/Collect_for_Purity for further translations of the original Latin prayer.

76 uk.businessinsider.com/difference-between-isis-and-al-qaeda-2015-5

77 See www.biography.com/news/john-lennon-imagine-song-facts for the full lyrics.

78 Billy Graham, *Peace with God* (Thomas Nelson, 1953), accessed via www.billygrahamlibrary.org/in-his-own-words-billy-graham-on-peace.

79 Robert Guelich, *Sermon on the Mount* (Word, 1982), p. 92.

80 See www.archives.gov/files/press/exhibits/dream-speech.pdf for the full speech.

81 www.christiantoday.com/article/nelson-mandela-and-his-faith/34956.htm

82 mg.co.za/article/2013-12-12-mandela-and-the-confessions-of-a-closet-christian

83 www.sahistory.org.za/article/speech-nelson-mandela-zionist-christian-church-easter-conference

84 www.ivpress.com/reconciling-all-things

85 www.amazon.co.uk/Cultivating-Peace-Becoming-21st-Century-Ambassador/dp/0984840710

86 faculty.georgetown.edu/jod/augustine/quote.html

87 www.premierchristianity.com/Past-Issues/2016/November-2016/The-Letter-of-Pete-Greig-to-the-UK-Church

88 en.wikipedia.org/wiki/Prayer_of_Saint_Francis

89 www.livius.org/sources/content/tacitus/tacitus-on-the-christians

90 Geoffrey Hanks, *70 Great Christians: Changing the world* (Christian Focus Publications Ltd, 1992), p. 16.

91 www.christian-history.org/letter-to-diognetus.html

92 Tim Dowley (ed.), *Handbook to the History of Christianity* (Eerdmans, 1977), p. 72.

93 Tertullian, *Apologeticus*, chapter 50.

94 Lactantius, *De Mortibus Persecutorum*, chapter 48.

95 www.pewforum.org/2011/12/19/global-christianity-regions

96 Brother Yun, *The Heavenly Man* (Monarch, 2002), p. 242.

97 www.opendoorsuk.org/persecution

98 www.cru.org/train-and-grow/spiritual-growth/prayer/pray-for-persecuted-church.html

99 See www.oxford.anglican.org/wp-content/uploads/2017/05/170517-Lazarus-1.pdf for the full transcript.

100 Stott, *Christian Counter-Culture*, p. 54.

101 www.hymnary.org/text/father_hear_the_prayer_we_offer_not_for

102 Stott, *Christian Counter-Culture*, p. 57.

103 en.oxforddictionaries.com/definition/the_salt_of_the_earth

104 www.thespiritlife.net/75-process/process-reflection/5249-reflections-from-john-stott

105 Charles E. Moore, 'Pandemic love', accessed via www.plough.com/en/topics/faith/discipleship/pandemic-love.

106 Hill, *The History of Christianity*, p. 427.

107 *Kirchliches Jahrbuch für die Evangelische Kirche in Deutschland*, 1933–44, p. 481.

108 Pastoral letter, 25 January 1941, A.B. Ermland, No. 2, 1 February 1941, pp. 13–14.

109 James Carroll, *Constantine's Sword* (Houghton Mifflin, 2002), pp. 271–72.

110 Hill, *The History of Christianity*, p. 427.

111 Hill, *The History of Christianity*, p. 427.

112 Dietrich Bonhoeffer, 'After ten years: a reckoning made at the New Year 1943' in Dietrich Bonhoeffer, *Letters and Papers from Prison* (Simon and Schuster, 1997).

113 Dietrich Bonhoeffer, *The Cost of Discipleship*, accessed via en.wikiquote.org/wiki/Dietrich_Bonhoeffer.

114 Payne Best, quoted in Dave Fleming, *Leadership Wisdom from Unlikely Voices* (Zondervan, 2004), p. 51.

115 Dorothy Sayers, 'Why work?', accessed via www.tnl.org/why-work-by-dorothy-sayers.

116 www.licc.org.uk/resources/discover-fruitfulness-on-the-frontline

117 www.foodgrainsbank.ca/uploads/Confession-%20Salt%20of%20the%20Earth.pdf

118 www.dailymail.co.uk/news/article-2848038/The-magical-job-Britain-Enchanting-story-gas-street-lights

119 Stephen Neil, *History of Christian Missions* (Penguin, 1990), p. 38.

120 www.pewresearch.org/fact-tank/2017/04/05

121 *The New York Times*, 8 November 1962, 'President Kennedy leads nation in expressing sorrow at death of Mrs. Roosevelt', p. 34, col. 1.

122 W. L. Watkinson, *The Supreme Conquest and Other Sermons Preached in America*, Sermon XIV: 'The invincible strategy' (Fleming H. Revell, 1907), pp. 217–18.

123 John Stott, *Issues Facing Christians Today* (Zondervan, 2006), pp. 63–79.

124 Stott, *Issues Facing Christians Today*, p. 67.

125 Robert Bellah in an interview in *Psychology Today* with Sam Green (January, 1976).

126 James Davison Hunter, *To Change the World* (Oxford University Press, 2010), p. 278.

127 Mary Bachelor (ed.), *The Lion Prayer Collection* (Lion Publishing, 1992), p. 66.

128 David Watson, *Discipleship* (Hodder and Stoughton, 1981), pp. 113–14.

129 David Watson, *You Are My God* (Hodder and Stoughton, 1983), p. 54.

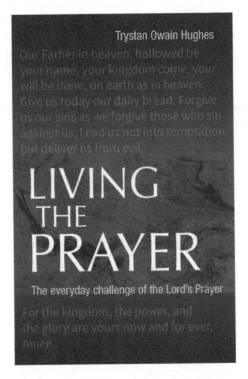

Trystan Owain Hughes

Our Father in heaven, hallowed be your name, your kingdom come, your will be done, on earth as in heaven. Give us today our daily bread. Forgive us our sins as we forgive those who sin against us. Lead us not into temptation but deliver us from evil.

LIVING THE PRAYER

The everyday challenge of the Lord's Prayer

For the kingdom, the power, and the glory are yours now and for ever. Amen.

Living the Prayer is a fresh perspective on the Lord's Prayer. Rooted in the Bible as well as in contemporary culture, it explores how this prayer can radically challenge and transform our daily lives. Contained in the prayer's 70 words is a fresh and innovative way of viewing, and acting in, the world that is as relevant now as it was 2,000 years ago. The author shows that this revolutionary prayer demands that we don't remain on our knees, but, rather, that we work towards making God's topsy-turvy, downside-up kingdom an everyday reality.

Living the Prayer
The everyday challenge of the Lord's Prayer
Trystan Owain Hughes
978 0 85746 623 5 £7.99

brfonline.org.uk

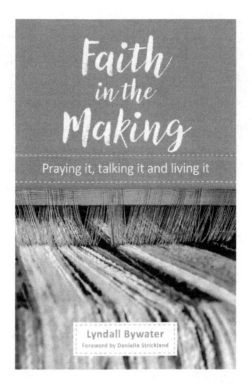

If 'faith is being sure of what we hope for and certain of what we do not see' what does that look like in practice today? In a world that is largely unsure and uncertain, how do we gain our confidence? *Faith in the Making* recognises the problem and seeks the answer in the list of faithful heroes found in Hebrews 11. This accessible, devotional resource will inspire individuals and groups to live more confidently for God in today's world. Heroic faith is far more attainable than we often think!

Faith in the Making
Praying it, talking it and living it
Lyndall Bywater
978 0 85746 555 9 £7.99

brfonline.org.uk

BRF

Transforming
lives and communities

Christian growth and understanding of the Bible

Resourcing individuals, groups and leaders in churches for their own spiritual journey and for their ministry

Church outreach in the local community

Offering three programmes that churches are embracing to great effect as they seek to engage with their local communities and transform lives

Teaching Christianity in primary schools

Working with children and teachers to explore Christianity creatively and confidently

Children's and family ministry

Working with churches and families to explore Christianity creatively and bring the Bible alive

Visit brf.org.uk for more information on BRF's work

brf.org.uk

The Bible Reading Fellowship (BRF) is a Registered Charity (No. 233280)